To Mrs. Rosalie Peck

whose love and passion for her community radiates through her eloquent words
and has inspired the entirety of this body of work.

A Master's Thesis Project by Sarah-Jane L. Vatelot

Chair:
Mark Weston

Committee:
Sergio DeSanto
Josue Robles Caraballo

Where have all the Mangoes gone?

Reactivating the Tropicana Field Site

On the Threshold of St Petersburg's History, Culture, and Memory

Spring 2019

University of South Florida School of Architecture and Community Design

3   Table of Contents

RESIDENTIAL

RAL ARTS DISTRICT

WATERFRONT ARTS DISTRICT

BAYFRONT
HOSPITAL
COMPLEX

EMENTARY
HOOL

UNIVERSITY

A Tear in the Fabric

7 Abstract

Tropicana Field is a baseball stadium, placed on 86 acres of land, located in the heart of St Petersburg, FL within walking distance from Downtown and its surrounding residential communities. The domed baseball stadium has made headlines since its construction in the 1980s and over the past year, the headline has been that the Tampa Bay Rays, the stadium's home team, are looking to build a new stadium across the bay, in Tampa, where they will garner more attendees and increase revenue.

Amid the buzz surrounding the Rays' potential departure and the future of the site, dwell the seldomly uttered stories of those who have witnessed the disappearance of their historic neighborhood. Previously named the Gas Plant neighborhood, after two towering gas cylinders which occupied the site, it was one of the areas first settled by African Americans in the late 19th century, many of whom were freely putting down their roots for the first time, in a new town which had yet to have a name.

The 20th century history of the African American community, particularly in the southern states, is a difficult one and can be characterized as one of resilience, perseverance, and triumph against the odds. Rosalie Peck, co-author of St Petersburg's Historic African American Neighborhoods and life-long resident of St Petersburg, offers that:

"One word defined St. Petersburg's historic African American neighborhoods: connectivity" (Peck & Wilson, 2008).

Currently, only one portion of the historic neighborhoods remains, around 9th Ave. S., the avenue of Faith, and 22nd St S., the street of Music. The three original settlements, Peppertown, Methodist Town and the Gas Plant no longer exist, having been walled off from the remainder of their community by the nearly unsurmountable highway. The disappearance of old neighborhoods in the name of urban renewal is nothing new and has been executed throughout history and across continents, some with great success and others without.

Tropicana Field has become an iconic building in St Petersburg's landscape. Many local baseball fans hold fond memories of watching their favorite teams play there. For many others, however, Tropicana Field is emblematic of a betrayal and of a persistent effort towards the erasure of their community. In light of current events, an unprecedented opportunity offers itself. The 86 acres of land which the Tropicana Field and its massive parking lot occupy, may now become available for re-development in its entirety and, in light of its painful history, it is incumbent upon the city to fulfill the broken promises which were once made to the African American community of St Petersburg, and to mend the tear in the city's urban fabric by developing site design features and implementing policies to guarantee inclusivity and re-establish continuity.

9   Research & Analysis

FREEDOM
IS THE NAME
OF
THE GAME

The Weekly Challenger

DISCOUNT FOODS GROCERIES MEATS COLD BEER SUNDRIES CLOTHING

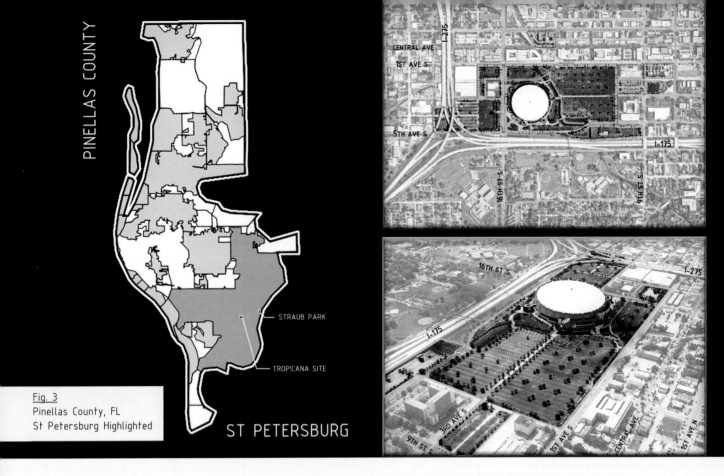

Fig. 3
Pinellas County, FL
St Petersburg Highlighted

ST PETERSBURG

11   Context

Site Information

Pinellas County is located on the West Coast of Florida with a population estimate of 970,637 (per 2017 US Census Bureau Estimate). St Petersburg sits on its southeastern edge with a population of 263,255 (per 2017 US Census Bureau Estimate). As apparent on the map above, the Tropicana Field Site is centrally located within St Petersburg's city limits.

The existing site encompasses 86 acres of land, or 3,750,000 sq. ft, and houses a multi-level 1,100,000 sq. ft. domed baseball stadium and over 6,000 parking spaces.

Construction began on Tropicana Field, formerly known as the Suncoast Dome, in 1986 (Walker, 1986) and was completed in March 1990 at an estimated cost of $138,000,000. (Brown, 2016)

Highway 275 and 175 line the site on its western and southern edges. Efforts to build the highway through St Petersburg began in 1970, met with much resistance from locals. The highway construction adjacent to the site was completed in 1980. (St Petersburg Times, 1980)

Fig 4
Florida Suncoast Dome under Construction – 1988

Site Observations

The site walk-through took place on Friday September 21st, 2018 beginning at 11am. The goal of the site visit was to record observations related to site access from the southside neighborhood. I began my journey at the Dr. Carter G. Woodson Museum of African American History near the intersection of 9th Ave S. and 22nd St. S. The goal was to experience the 2 different access routes which I had identified on the map, due to the barrier imposed by the highway. I chose to access the site walking north on 22nd St S.

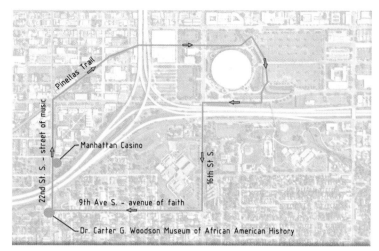

I stopped at the historic Manhattan Casino which gave 22nd St S. its nickname as the Street of Music. I inquired within and was invited upstairs for a visit. The Manhattan Casino is an event space which was affectionately called "the home of happy feet". (Peck & Wilson, 2006) The likes of Ray Charles, Louis Armstrong, James Brown, Sarah Vaughn and Duke Ellington graced this venue with their soulful music and powerful voices. There was an undeniable energy in the beautifully renovated dance hall.

Fig. 5
The Manhattan Casino

For a moment, I could almost hear the "searing blues notes pelting out the Manhattan's open windows." (Peck & Wilson, 2006).

It was a social center, "a haven for music lovers and an undisputed escape from daily hardship and racial scorn." (Peck & Wilson, 2006) The significance of this building was not lost on me, as well its situation, severed by the highway from the community which it serves.

I continued my journey north on 22nd St. S. to the Pinellas trail upon which I made a right and followed it to the site. This portion of the walk was long; passing buildings which don't particularly address the street, warehouses and their disagreeable noises, and passing under the highway again prompting my arrival to the site. As the images illustrate, I did not encounter a single pedestrian along the way.

13   Tropicana Field comes alive when there is a baseball game, otherwise, it is an empty landscape.

I did not venture onto the parking lot. I could see the heat rising from its surface and chose to walk along Booker Creek instead. The creek appears to be an afterthought. Once polluted by the adjacent gas plant, it was still used by children as a place to cool down on a hot day. In my interview with Reverend Watson Haynes, head of the Urban League in St Petersburg and an accomplished community leader, he recalled swimming in the creek and climbing the gas cylinders to enjoy a panoramic view of the city, as a young boy. The walk along the creek was pleasant, with the sound of the water providing welcome relief from the industrial and highway noise which had accompanied me to the site. I noted a few turtles and fish swimming by.

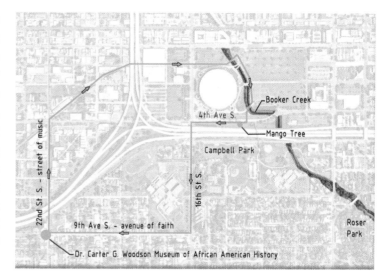

The topography is noteworthy, in flat St Petersburg. The parking lot slopes gently towards the creek, while the change in elevation is more picturesque nearing the stadium, with what appears to be at least a 25-30-foot differential near the wooden bridge, on the north end of the site. This landscape is an echo of Roser Park, just half of a mile down the creek, a small residential neighborhood with curved brick paved streets and hilltop homes. It is considered a hidden gem of St Petersburg, its first "streetcar suburb". (Wright, 2014). As I followed the creek, I encountered 4th Avenue S. which lines Highway 175. I crossed the street and walked west towards 16th St S.

Then I saw a large mango tree, trapped between the highway and a chain-link fence.

The mango tree appears to carry with it a memory of place and time.

I continued past the mango tree and turned left onto 16th St. S., under the highway again. On the other side, I passed Campbell Park, with its sports fields, playground, and exercise area. The street here begins to liven with the sounds of children playing, and passersby conversing. As I turned right onto 9th Ave. S., I passed more pedestrians and bike riders. I heard music streaming out of nearby homes. The street is lined with churches and placards elaborating on the history of the Avenue of Faith. The avenue looks unpolished, but it has spirit.

The walk back to 22nd St S. felt pleasant despite the heat.

Fig 6.
Dr. Carter G. Woodson Museum of African American History

I arrived at the Carter G. Woodson Museum of African American History. The building used to serve as the administrative office for adjacent Jordan Park. "In 1937, the St. Petersburg City Council authorized a housing authority" (Wilson, 2014) due to substandard living conditions in parts of Peppertown, Methodist Town, and the Gas Plant neighborhood. The last phase of Jordan Park was completed by 1941 and offered over 400 homes. Jordan Park was a great success. The homes were built by people of the community for the community. Many families have lived in these homes until they could afford to purchase or build their own homes.

Upon entering the museum, I met with volunteer Lynette Hardy who shared her story with me. Her grandfather was Chester James, the unofficial mayor of Methodist Town, who advocated for his neighborhood with such passion that Methodist Town was also named Jamestown in his honor. She shared that Jordan park provided people with a "feeling of ownership and identity". She related to me that some people from the Southside St Petersburg African American community still do not feel welcome downtown. There is history associated with this feeling.

15

She took me to the legacy gardens behind the museum and recalled "plaiting the maypole" there as a young girl, a dance performed as a celebration of Emancipation Day in Florida on May 20th.

The legacy garden was founded in 2008. Two large oak trees cast merciful shade onto the garden. The temperature difference was striking. 200 Magnolia were shipped from Georgia and over 2000 plants grace the garden. The names of those who contributed to the garden are engraved in the brick pavers. The garden is currently enjoyed by museumgoers and rented as an event space.

Mrs. Hardy shared with me that many people said the garden wouldn't thrive due to the summer heat.

Fig 7.
Children plaiting the Maypole in St Petersburg

"Love and prayer fed the garden", she told me.

The garden felt like an oasis, after a long walk in the heat, a beautiful extension of the museum and place to celebrate.

The site walk-through was informative and led me to establish that, of the two routes I had chosen to take, the 16th St S. route is the most logical point of access to the site from the adjacent Southside neighborhood. Although the neighborhood was razed over 30 years ago, the land still bears witness to its history, which carries on among its people.

The question comes to mind: Why is this story different?

I was invited to attend a meeting at the St Petersburg Chamber of Commerce with a group entitled Grow Smarter, which is comprised of concerned professionals (developers, representatives of nearby districts and organizations). Everyone there was full of great intentions to ensure that the site be developed with everyone's best interest in mind. Meeting participants introduced themselves and provided a synopsis of their organization and interest in the future of the site. Mrs. Veatrice Farrell introduced herself as the program manager of the Deuces Live, a non-profit organization dedicated to creating "an atmosphere within the historic 22nd Street South District that both stimulates new growth and enhances the current commercial/residential population". She reminded everyone that this "site" had been home to hundreds of people, businesses, churches, a library, schools, and graveyards. The room fell silent. I observed the uncomfortable and quiet acknowledgment of what had just been said, and the meeting moved forward. This moment was pivotal in my understanding of the real issue with the site. Some see the potential in this space, while others fondly remember their lives in this place.

Population displacement is nothing new, and an unfortunate side effect of urban renewal. Something different exists in this narrative and I was determined to understand it better. I approached Mrs. Farrell and asked for her advice. She gave me the names of people whom she knew that I should contact for interviews. I was thankful for her meaningful interjection.

17   History

Initial research into the site led me to many history books chronicling St Petersburg's founding and growth through the 20th century. In some, the gas plant and the neighborhood surrounding it were mentioned. Others detailed some of the historic incidences tied to St Petersburg's history of racial segregation, many of which occurred on the site as it resides in tension on the edge of the area historically occupied by African Americans. Once I arrived upon Mrs. Rosalie Peck and Jon Wilson's St Petersburg's Historic African American Neighborhoods and St Petersburg's Historic 22nd St S., I knew had found the voice I had been searching for.

Mrs. Farrell had provided me with contact information for author Jon Wilson citing him as a good source of information. I was fortunate to meet with him at his University of South Florida office in St Petersburg. Mr. Wilson is a historian who has written extensively about St Petersburg's history. He shared with me that Mrs. Rosalie Peck had approached him in the early 2000s, expressing the need for her community's history, much of which had been preserved orally, to be written, not to be forgotten. Her contemporaries were passing on and her desire was to tell a story which the history books did not.

Fig 8.
Jon Wilson and Rosalie Peck

After reading their books, cover to cover, I felt compelled to reconstruct this history.

To fully understand Mrs. Peck's thesis, that connectivity defined St Petersburg's historic African American neighborhoods, I identified the site on a map dating to 1947, as shown below. The highway is absent, and the urban fabric is continuous. The only indication of a physical barrier denoted on this map are the railroad tracks, which have historically served as "iron barriers of race and class." (Badger, 2015). African American Railroad workers settled the site in the late 19th century while constructing "a lifeline towards the dusty paths and few frail buildings that comprised a hamlet still without a name" (Peck & Wilson, 2008).

The railroad, named the Orange Belt Railway, originated in Central Florida and ended in St Petersburg, connecting the St John's River to Tampa Bay (Hensley, 2011).

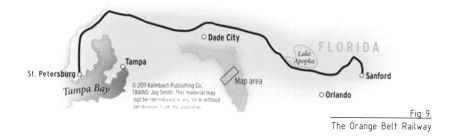

Fig 9.
The Orange Belt Railway

The completion of the railroad in 1888 arguably marked the birth of St Petersburg as a town. The first African Americans to arrive in numbers were the "men of the Orange Belt" (Peck & Wilson, 2008). Upon the completion of the railroad in 1888 some stayed and settled what came to be known as Peppertown. Unlike what may be assumed, Peppertown derived its name from its residents growing "peppers of all kinds in their yards" (Peck & Wilson, 2008). In 1894, Methodist Town began to grow in, what were at the time, "the western reaches of downtown St Petersburg" (Peck & Wilson, 2008). It stood its ground as the only African American Neighborhood north of the railroad for many years until most of its residents were displaced in the 1970s. The Gas Plant neighborhood grew simultaneously, originally named Cooper's Quarters.

"May they rediscover the old ties - may they learn what these ties meant and how important they were.

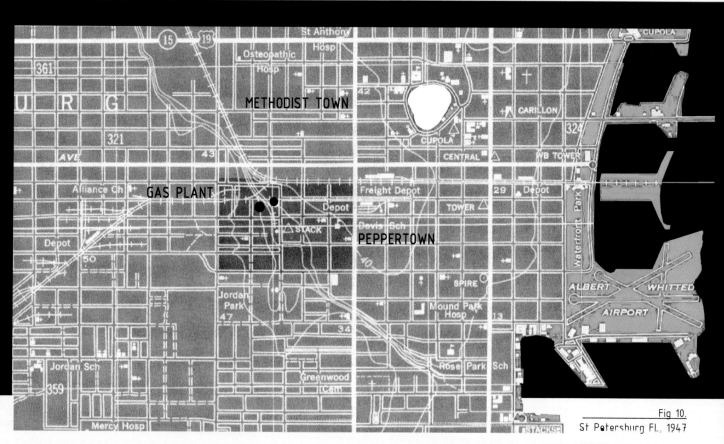

Fig 10.
St Petersburg FL, 1947

And may they forge a new and revised sense of community connection as the new century unfolds." (Peck & Wilson, 2008)

The master plan proposals currently put forward by HKS Architects and the City of St Petersburg have given the name to the proposed development as the Gas Plant District. Although this name was given to the site in the past, it was done so, largely, because the gas plant was the economic interest that the city had with the neighborhood, at the time.

Mr. Wilson and Mrs. Peck described the Gas Plant neighborhood otherwise, as "a densely packed residential and business area with each court and enclave bearing its own name, but in general was called the Gas Plant because of two skyline huge cylinders that stored the city's natural gas supply." (Peck & Wilson, 2008). Rev. Watson Haynes assisted me in locating some of the enclaves described by Mrs. Peck, with whom he had shared a close friendship. He indicated that there was overlap among these areas and their boundaries were loosely defined. He listed others: Founder's Court, Lilly Court, Forty Quarters, the Hollow and Lincoln Court. On the map below, I located Little Egypt, Jamestown, Cooper's Quarters and Sugar Hill as I also found corroborating evidence of their more precise locations within the literature. Rev. Haynes also related to me that the names of the areas which had a proper name followed by "court" or "quarters" were named so after the white land owners. Although I did not locate any images of it, the most vividly described sub-neighborhood is Sugar Hill. Located on the site were Davis Academy: the first African American school in St Petersburg, the first medical treatment facility for African Americans in St Petersburg, the first library for African Americans, the Harlem Theater, 13 churches, cemeteries, locally owned businesses and hundreds of residents. (Peck & Wilson, 2008)

The images, pinpointed onto the map below, assist in adding a built dimension to the map. Understanding the urban and social fabric in the third dimension is critical to understanding it at the human scale.

19 "Mittie Walton Pounds remembers: "Oh yes, the scary gas tanks were there but the neighborhood within a neighborhood that I grew up in, in the shadow of those big old tanks, was known as Little Egypt." (Peck & Wilson, 2008)

This map attempts to locate some of the enclaves within the Gas Plant neighborhood and reconstitute some of its physical and social fabric.

Sugar Hill, "probably named for its counterpart in New York City's Harlem" (Peck & Wilson, 2008), was located just north of Campbell Park, on the southern edge of the Gas Plant neighborhood, where highway 175 currently resides.

"It was a neighborhood within a neighborhood, and its few gracious dwellings represented aspiration and attainment. In majestic stone mansions, stately brick dwellings, and well-kept bungalows lived the elite society of St Petersburg's influential black families, and the area was the pride of St Petersburg's African American population." (Peck & Wilson, 2008)

"On that paved and lighted roadway lived doctors, funeral directors and educators. They served as role models for children - and even younger adults striving to make their way - who often lived in lesser circumstances just a short walk away in enclaves such as Little Egypt, Forty Quarters, and the Hollow" (Peck & Wilson, 2008) The residents of the area recall it fondly rising as "a sweet vision of success".... "For the rest of the black community, 5th Ave S., without a doubt, stood as an oasis of hope for the less fortunate citizens stranded in an apparently endless desert of race-based segregation." (Peck & Wilson, 2008).

I visited the Lakeview Market on 22nd Ave S, where I had been told that I could find the Swintons, who had run a store in the Gas Plant neighborhood. I found Mrs. Daisy Swinton there and she kindly shared her story. She had run a store in the Gas Plant neighborhood, much like the one she owns today. She still bakes the same delicious pies which she was known for in the 1970s. She worked across the street from where she lived.

Fig. 11.
Lakeview Market

"That dome took my home" she said.

She related to me that the greatest loss that people suffered was economic. The elderly can't get around, she explained. They like to walk. After the Gas Plant neighborhood was gone, it was more difficult for them to shop. Although she was able to relocate her store, many businesses, which had been handed down from previous generations, did not succeed in doing so. Mrs. Willie Mae Grayson owned Bill's RonRico Club, a thriving bar and hotel located along 2nd Ave S. "They told her they were going to build up around there, and she was very jubilant -- very happy for that... She had her whole building remodeled thinking they were going to upgrade the community and she would be there." (Glasser, 2018) In 1985, Mrs. Grayson was made to sell her property due to the city's exercise of eminent domain, "when her building was demolished, Willie Mae's spirit...was also crushed." (Glasser, 2018).

Mrs. Peck and Mr. Wilson compiled a list of the businesses and churches present in the Gas Plant at the time of its razing.

Businesses:
Harlem Theater, Harlem Cafe, Citizen's Lunch Counter, Cozy Corner Night Club, Katz Groceries, Bill's Ron Rico Club, Central Life Insurance, Selena's Beauty Salon, Kilgore's drugs, Jay's Pharmacy, Eddie's Shoe Shine, Laurence Clark Confections, Hick's Service Station, B&B Luncheonette, Morton's Restaurant, and Newkirk's Steakhouse.

Churches:
Antioch Baptist, Bethel Metropolitan Baptist, First Baptist Institutional, Galilee Missionary Baptist, Prayer Tower Church of God in Christ, Second Bethel Baptist, Saint Augustine Episcopal, McCabe Memorial Methodist.

Mrs. Swinton's store is the only one I could locate which is currently operating. Of the 13 churches which existed on the site at the time of displacement, I was able to locate all of them on the map.

Still the question remains, why are these neighborhoods gone and why does it matter?

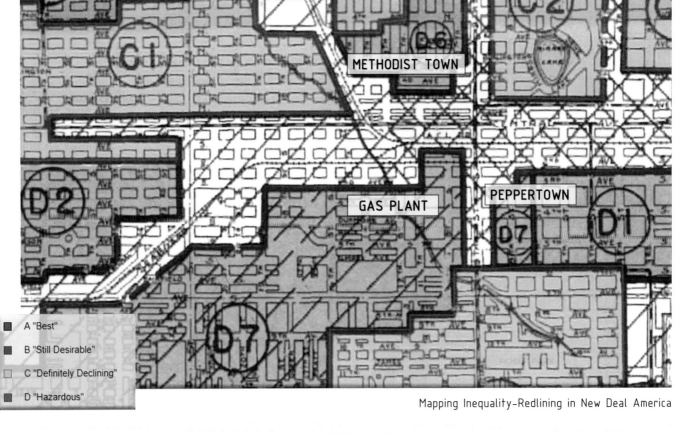

Mapping Inequality-Redlining in New Deal America

21   "Had I understood that you intended to take my home I would have never voted for it.

It is important to consider the cause for displacement of the populations of Peppertown, Methodist Town, and the Gas Plant because it is part of a trajectory which the city embarked upon in the 1930s. When the neighborhoods were first settled, African Americans grouped together out of convenience and safety. Racial segregation didn't truly become a matter of policy until the 1930s directly resulting from the Great Depression of 1929. The Home Owner's Loan Corporation (HOLC) drafted "Security Maps", as shown above, in the 1930s, which developers, realtors, tax assessors, surveyors and municipalities accessed to assist in devising strategies for economic recovery. Among the considerations that qualified a neighborhood as "hazardous" or "declining" was the proximity to or demarcation as a "negro section". One decision which resulted from the compiling of these security maps was the city's 1935 "Proposed Negro Segregation Project", as shown top right, in which a legal description is provided for the relocation of African Americans who were deemed to be located within too close of a proximity to Downtown. In an effort to clean up Downtown's image, to be more appealing to tourists, the residents of Methodist Town, Peppertown and the Gas Plant would need to be relocated.

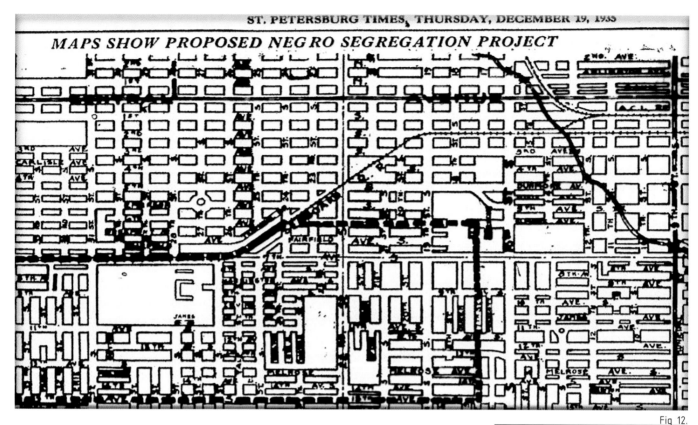

MAPS SHOW PROPOSED NEGRO SEGREGATION PROJECT

Fig 12.
Proposed Negro Segregation Project, 1935

I have never, never, never wanted to get rid of it...We've got nice homes here."– Chester James (Phelps, 1975)

The completion of Jordan Park in 1941, which was located within the confines of the segregation project's boundaries, heralded the disappearance of Peppertown as most of its residents relocated there.

Methodist Town was cleared out of most of its residents in the 1970s. Chester James, Mrs. Hardy's grandfather, was a strong advocate for his neighborhood, Methodist Town. For years, "he lobbied city hall to improve dark unpaved streets and to crack down on landlords who neglected the housing they rented to families." (Peck, & Wilson, 2008) It is worthy of mention that the HOLC map descriptions of "detrimental influences" (pictured left) listed "dilapidated repair conditions of the majority of properties" in Methodist Town, laying blame on the tenants. Mr. James' lobbying efforts for the city to crack down on landlords who neglected their rental properties, provides a contrasting narrative. In 1974, he was named the neighborhood's honorary mayor by the city council and it was renamed Jamestown in his honor. That same year, Mr. James worked with the city to redevelop the neighborhood, which, he was led to believe, would bring much needed improvements for its residents. Instead, "it resulted in the relocation of 377 families" (Peck & Wilson, 2008). Jon Wilson was present at the city council meeting as a young reporter for the St Petersburg Times when Chester James "waved his cane" in anger at the city council, who, it can be said, had used him to achieve their ends.

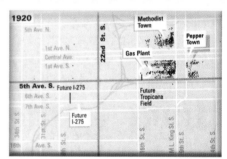

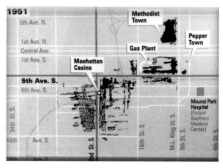

Fig 13
Maps tracing the concentrations and growth of St Petersburg's African American communities

Then the Gas Plant would be razed in the 1980s under similar pretexts of community redevelopment.

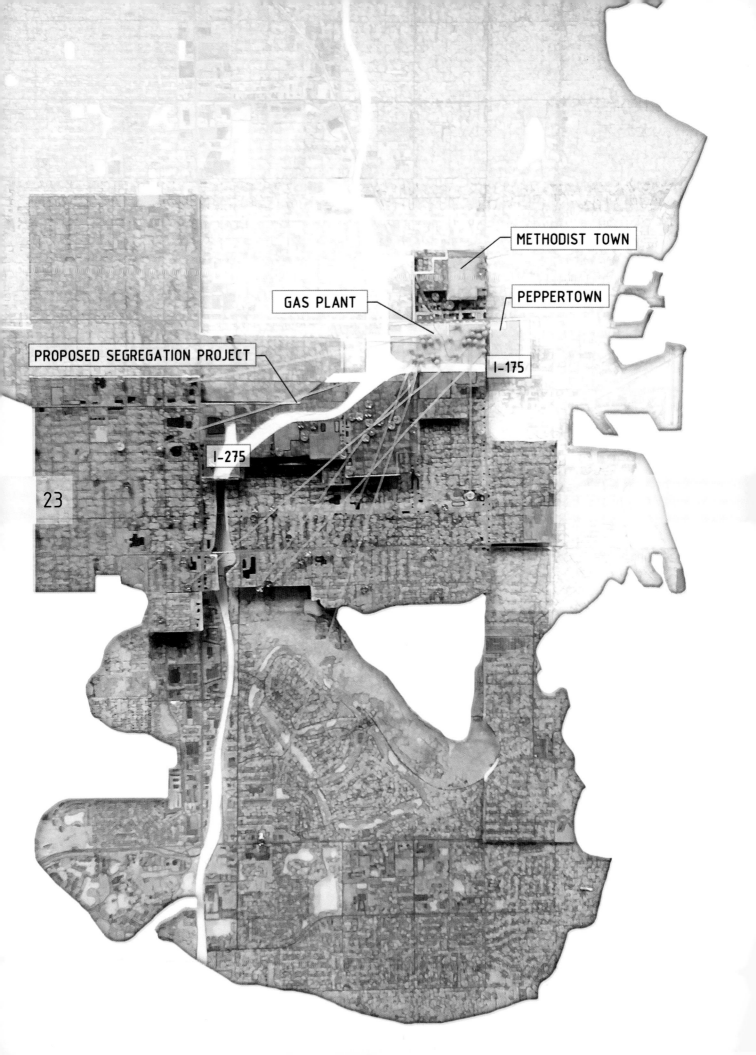

METHODIST TOWN

GAS PLANT

PEPPERTOWN

PROPOSED SEGREGATION PROJECT

I-175

I-275

23

The map to the left includes several layers of information that, when compiled into a single map, visually illustrates St Petersburg's physical legacy of segregation and displacement. The shades of blue denote the concentration of African American residents according to the 2010 Census. The darkest blue color indicates a concentration of over 80% African American, whereas the lightest color on the map indicates a concentration of less than 20% African American. Even though the civil rights movement put an end to racial segregation in the 1960s, its boundaries remain strikingly visible. Above highway I-175, the HOLC security map boundaries are shown for Methodist Town, Peppertown and the Gas Plant, overlain with the concentration of African American residents. Interestingly, Methodist Town is shown to still have over 40% African American residents, even through 377 families were displaced in the mid-1970s. The area in relief to the southwest of I-175 with I-275 slicing through it shows the legal description boundary for the city's 1935 proposed segregation project. Although they were never able to fully enforce this boundary, the intention to move African American residents away from Downtown was mostly realized, as recently as the 1980s. While there is little evidence that, in the 1980s, the deliberate intent was to conclude the efforts begun in the 1930s, the goal was fulfilled, and it was not helpful that the residents of the Gas Plant were promised in writing that the neighborhood would be rebuilt with "new, affordable housing and a modern-day industrial park. The plan also promised in writing 600 new jobs, with combined salaries of $5.6-million, by the end of the 1980s." (Harper, 1998)

"This change disrupted the continuity in people's lives. Tenements and shacks disappeared but so did the fine homes in places like Sugar Hill where the elegant Ponder Home and its beloved cherry hedge disappeared." (Peck & Wilson, 2008)

"No other project caused the degree of resentment that the gas plant bulldozing did. Part of it was because residents there had believed that renewal of another kind was coming." (Peck & Wilson, 2008)

LEGEND

 > 80% African American

 > 60% African American

 > 40% African American

 > 20% African American

 < 20% African American

 Business or church location in the Gas Plant area

Current church location in the > 80% African American portion of the southside neighborhood

Baseball was not in the original plan, nor is it connected to the land. The neighborhood was "declared a redevelopment area by City Council on September 7, 1978.... Initially envisioned to support an industrial park and residential development." according to Council Resolution 78-738. In 1986, six city council members voted to build the stadium on the site rather than allowing it to go for a referendum (Nickens, 2016). By this time, the city had spent "$11.3-million, about $2-million more than originally budgeted" (Harper, 1998) on the acquisition of land and demolition of the neighborhood. The funds came from "federal community redevelopment grants, which were supposed to help lift people out of poverty" (Harper, 1998). With a total price-tag of $138,000,000 for taxpayers the Suncoast Dome was built, and the promise of economic development tied to the stadium's draw has yet to be fulfilled. Then Secretary of Education, Douglas L. Jamerson, whose grandmother had lived in the neighborhood stated that "Obviously [he does] not think the promises made (when the Gas Plant was leveled) have been kept, and [he thinks] the failure to keep faith with the commitments made to the people has been part of the underpinnings of the tension that has taken place in St. Petersburg". (Harper, 1998) It was another broken promise and the realization of a 50-year project.

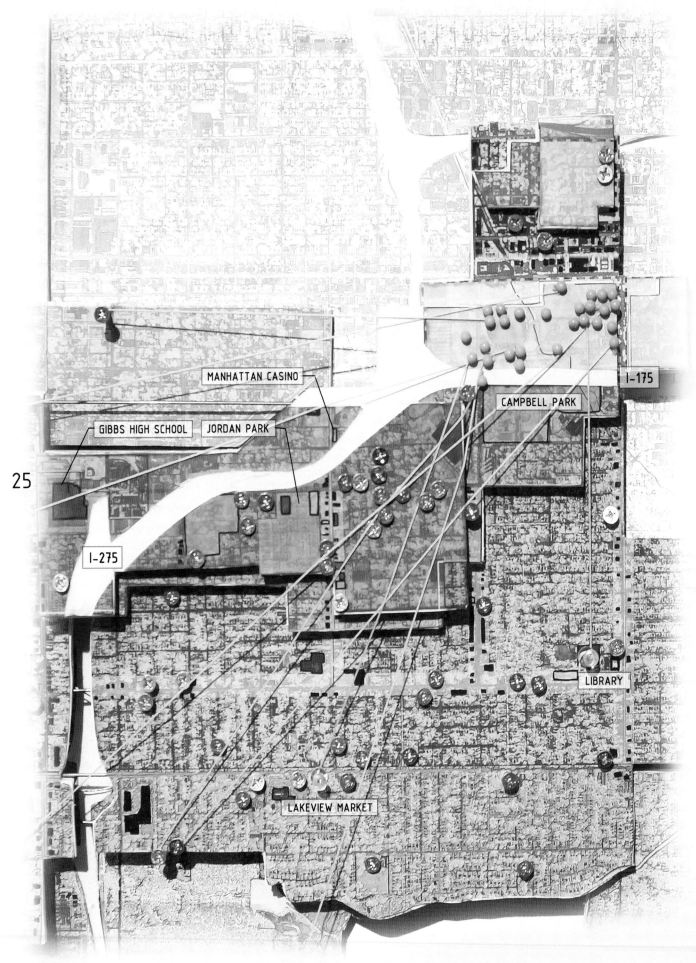

MANHATTAN CASINO

GIBBS HIGH SCHOOL   JORDAN PARK

CAMPBELL PARK

I-175

I-275

LIBRARY

LAKEVIEW MARKET

Social Capital and Legacy of Segregation and Displacement

The other remarkable boundary on the map is the highway, shown slicing through the heart of the community, severing from its core residential areas, Gibbs High School, which was directly connected to Campbell Park through 9th Ave S., and the Manhattan Casino. When the highway was under construction in the late 1970s, the Gas Plant neighborhood was effectively severed off from the rest of the community. Highway 175 was built directly over "the gracious dwellings" of Sugar Hill, and this violent act marked the beginning of the end of the Gas Plant neighborhood. Between 9th Ave. N and 5th Ave. S the highway is porous, whereas when it reaches the blue areas shown on the map, it becomes a wall with few points of crossing, leaving on its edge countless dead-end streets.

Sarah Schindler writes in her article Architectural Exclusion: Discrimination and Segregation Through Physical Design of the Built Environment, in the Yale Law Journal that "the placement of highways so as to intentionally displace poor black neighborhoods is even more familiar. Policymakers purposefully decided to route highways through the center of cities, often with the intent to destroy low-income and especially black neighborhoods in an effort to reshape the physical and racial landscapes of the postwar American city. Although this work was undertaken in order to make places more accessible to cars, it was also done with an eye towards eliminating alleged slums and blight in city centers. These tactics were so common that they earned a name among critics: "white roads through black bedrooms."" (Schindler, 2015)

The yellow pins on the map represent the existing churches and businesses at the time that the neighborhood was demolished. The thread leads to the site of relocation of the churches, Mrs. Swinton's Lakeview Market and the James Weldon Johnson Community Library. The map illustrates the southwestern exodus which occurred from the site.

Another layer of information on the map is the social capital of the community. The existing locally owned businesses were darkened on the map as well as the schools and institutions serving the community. The screws on the map, physically holding the layers of history together, are the churches. The number of churches in the over 80% African American area is striking. Church institutions have historically held prominent positions within African American culture.

"Churches provided a stable and empowering social experience, more than any other institution. Churches helped newcomers find homes and jobs. They fed and clothed the poor when other institutions would not. They combined their influence to speak to the white establishment downtown." (Peck & Wilson, 2008)

The question now becomes, who has the right to the city? While certain neighborhoods receive the distinction of being named historic districts, why were Methodist Town, Peppertown and the Gas Plant treated differently? The answer to this question is self-evident, in light of our history. There has been a blatant institutionalized bias elevating one culture over all others. The Gas Plant, in particular, had buildings of historical significance gracing its site; buildings built at the turn of the 20th century, some of architectural significance such as the church built of seashells referred to as "Shell Dash" (Peck & Wilson, 2008), but mostly the significance was cultural.

David Harvey, in his manifesto for urban social justice, The Right to the City, calls this process of displacement "accumulation by dispossession, giving rise to all manner of conflicts over the capture of high value land from low income populations that may have lived there for many years." The residents and business owners were compensated for their displacement but the "sense of community" which Rev. Haynes speaks of, the sense of continuity, permanence and historic belonging were taken and those attributes are irreplaceable. The event which occurred was effectively an erasure of a historically marginalized people's local culture and history, whose right to the city needs to equal that of other residents. This right is "far more than a right of individual access to the resources that the city embodies: it is a right to change ourselves by changing the city more after our heart's desire. It is, moreover, a collective rather than an individual right since changing the city inevitably depends upon the exercise of a collective power over the processes of urbanization." (Harvey, 2003).

In light of this history, it is absolutely critical to move forward with an awareness of the past, to construct an inclusive future for our city and to implement design strategies in the redevelopment of the site which allow people to re-enter the site, regain a sense of local ownership, and thrive.

"The freedom to make and remake ourselves and our cities is, I want to argue, one of the most precious yet most neglected of our human rights." (Harvey, 2003)

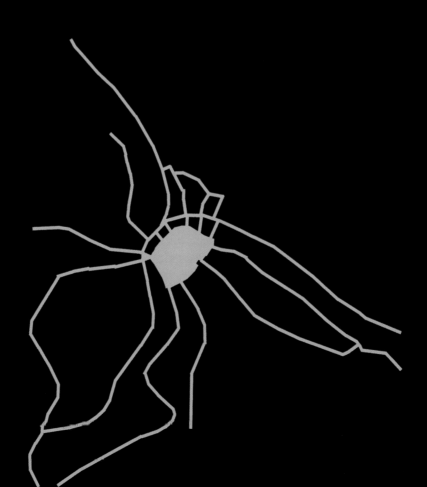

In August 2018, I was invited to participate in a 2-day Design Charette sponsored by local architecture firm Renker Eich Parks Architects, local developer Feldman Equities, and local general contacting firm Bandes Construction. I was part of a design team comprised of Maisey Rawe, Olivia Leamer, and Savannah Moller. After a cursory review of the site and noting the void left in the urban fabric, the team settled on the idea that the design of the site should enhance Booker Creek and include an urban plaza as its main feature connected to Campbell Park by a land bridge.

St Petersburg does not have an urban plaza. The waterfront is uniquely adorned with a 7-mile stretch of parks, a gesture mandated early on, by the city's founders Peter Demens, William Straub and Perry Snell, in the spirit of the city beautiful movement which had gained popularity in the early 20th century as a refute to the squalid urban conditions left in many city centers in the wake of industrialization.

Fig 14.
Straub Park, St. Petersburg

Although St Petersburg thrives on it edges, most of its population lives in its center. The place where residents currently gather to celebrate is Straub Park, the waterfront park which has defaulted as its city's plaza. A city plaza has different qualities than a park and St Petersburg would benefit from the intensity which a well-designed plaza could bring to the area. During the charette, the urban plaza idea was given the name of Urban Beach. In contrast to a park which showcases nature in an unnatural place, in an urban plaza "citizens are not connected to manifestations of nature, but to the heart of urban culture, history and memory". (Levy, 2012)

To support this hypothesis, I have identified urban plazas which have successfully enhanced their public realm and, in many cases, have been urban catalysts for redevelopment and community well-being. I have drawn 1 sq. km. of their figure-ground with the public space highlighted in yellow. Per the Project for Public Spaces, a successful public space operates with the "tentacles of an octopus, extending into the surrounding neighborhood". The public plaza's "octopus" was then drawn to identify the extent and efficacy of its reach into the surrounding urban fabric.

"On a square, citizens are not connected to manifestations of nature, but to the heart of urban culture, history and memory"

The beautiful Piazza del Campo in Siena, Italy, has inspired the concept of Urban Beach. It is arguably one of the most successful public plazas in the world for the manner in which it serves and connects its community. It has been called an urban beach because of the way people sit and lounge upon its sloped surface. In this place, residents, tourists, and visitors do not come to see a body of water or other natural feature, they come for the architecture, they come to see and to be seen. The mixed-use buildings frame the space and have a porosity which allows for pedestrian access, from many directions, and spectacular view corridors. The plaza's open plan provides "flexibility in the types of activities that occur in the space. Public performances and other informal activities often occur in the center of the square because the downward slope of the space creates a natural amphitheater for spectators." (D'Alessio, 2016) The grand open space allows for spontaneous and planned activities of varying scale. The edge of the space is activated by the presence of museums, retail spaces, restaurants and cafes on the ground level. The upper floors house residential, office, and civic uses. The success of such spaces lies in their programming. Unlike a park, which is relatively unsafe to venture into at night, due to the absence of eyes on the space, a plaza can be programmed to have eyes and ears on it at all times. Siena was built around this public space and it serves as a connector between its surrounding neighborhoods. Piazza del Campo provides its residents with a sense of identity and its tentacles reach far into its urban fabric, quite gracefully.

Piazza del Campo, Italy
Population: 53,000

Fig 15.
Piazza del Campo, Sienna

Portsmouth Square is a historic town square dating back to the time when San Francisco was first settled and named Yerba Buena. The city of San Francisco was founded around the square which was the center of public life in the 19th century. In quickly densifying 20th Century San Francisco, the square lost its importance and was turned into a parking lot in the 1960s. It was redesigned as a public square atop a parking garage in the 1990s and is now referred to as "the heart of Chinatown". Its success is due to its "contemporary and inclusive design that caters both to the general public while including elements that make it a culturally significant space for local Chinese Americans." (Project for Public Places) The square's redevelopment has reinvigorated the surrounding community and provided a place of connection and repose.

The figure ground illustrates the dense surrounding urban fabric and small walkable block sizes of San Francisco. The octopus reflects its tight grid.

Portsmouth Square, San Francisco, CA Population: 884,363

Campus Martius, Detroit MI Population: 677,116

Fig 16. Portsmouth Square

Fig 17. Campus Martius

Campus Martius in downtown Detroit is a successful example of the establishment of an urban plaza acting as a catalyst for urban regeneration. After decades of decline, the city took pro-active steps towards re-activating its urban core starting with the creation of a park in the heart of downtown. "Campus Martius Park opened in November 2004, people started coming back downtown for concerts, outdoor movies, the ever-changing flower gardens, dates at the park cafe, or simply to sit and relax by the fountain." Of note, the presence of the plaza "became a key factor in the decision of Compuware, a software company, to move its 3,500 employees downtown... into a new $400,000,000 building on the park—a reversal of longstanding patterns of businesses fleeing the city." (Project for Public Places) This move set off a chain reaction which inspired investors to renovate surrounding buildings to welcome new tenants.

The plaza's tentacles reach into the surrounding urban fabric and effectively create a sense of destination.

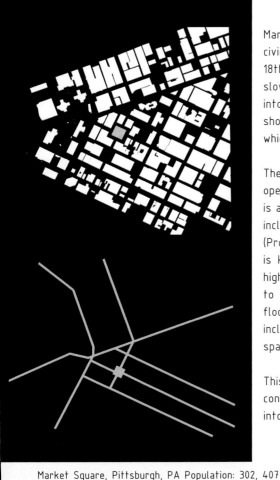

Market Square, which had been the center of civic and public life in Pittsburgh since the 18th century, "had been in a 50 year cycle of slow decay." when in 2009, it was remodeled into "a European-style plaza for dining, shopping, business meetings and leisure." which successfully rejuvenated the area.

The morphology of the square as a 1.1-acre open plaza affords it flexibility in use, while it is activated on its edges by "first floor retail including restaurants and sidewalk cafés." (Project for Public Places) Use in the area is key. Adjacent uses to the square include, high-rise buildings serving as headquarters to global corporations and use of the upper floors of the immediate surrounding buildings include living units and commercial office space.

This mixture of surrounding uses ensures a continuity of use throughout the day and well into the evening.

Market Square, Pittsburgh, PA Population: 302, 407

Discovery Green, Houston TX Population: 2,296,224

Fig 18. Market Square

Fig 19. Discovery greeen

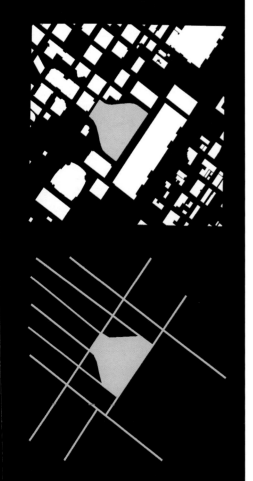

Discovery Green, also known as "Houston's backyard", is more of a traditional park space than the previous studies. Prior to its opening in 2008, "Downtown Houston had long been characterized as a district of office towers. "The streets felt like concrete canyons," ..." (Project for Public Spaces)

The relevance of this case study is its adjacency to Houston's convention center, which acts as an activator of the park. The programing of the park is another one of its successful features. "Discovery Green's 12 acres encompass 11 gardens, 4 water features, 2 restaurants, 2 outdoor catered-event areas, 2 outdoor market areas, a stage, 2 dog runs and fountains, 2 bocce ball courts, 2 outdoor library reading rooms with library services and wi-fi, a putting green, a playground, a jogging trail, and a shuffleboard court." (Project for Public Places)

Houston is not known for its walkability, yet Discovery Green has reached into its surrounding fabric and activated its public realm.

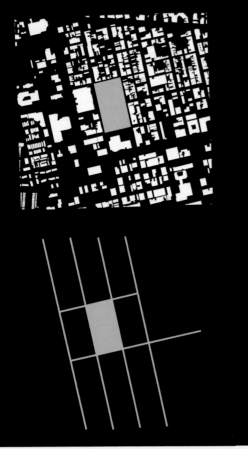

Washington Square Park is an interesting case study due to its context. Over-the-Rhine is a neighborhood in Cincinnati "with a very troubled recent past, at one time being saddled with the dubious distinction of being called the most crime ridden neighborhood in the country." (Benfield, 2012) This was a result of a dramatic population decrease during the 1920s which led to high rates of building vacancies, poverty and crime, all due to "deterioration, neglect, and poor public policy." (Benfield, 2012) The 150-year-old park was renovated in 2012 with the philosophy that "every neighborhood needs a center - a civic space where its residents and visitors can come together, enjoy well-maintained amenities and feel safe" (Benfield, 2012)

The city is putting special care into not only revitalizing the historic neighborhood but developing strategies to help avoid gentrifying the area by putting policies in place which will assist in keeping its existing residents, while inviting new ones to grow the community...

Washington Square Park, Cincinnati, OH Population: 301,301
Cheonoggyecheon Stream Park, Seoul, South Korea Population: 9,776,000

Fig 20 Washington Square Park
Fig 21. Cheonoggyecheon Stream Park

Cheonoggyecheon Stream Park in Seoul, South Korea was opened in 2005 and lauded as a successful project in urban renewal. "In 1968, an elevated highway was built over the stream which led it to almost dry up." This highway also divided Seoul into northern and southern sections. The stream's restoration transformed a highway barrier into a space of juncture between the two neighborhoods. The stream's refurbishment led to a revitalization of the area directly around it encouraging shops, restaurants and amenities to open and further improve the public realm.

The stream provides a waterside promenade, moments to pause, spaces to gather and celebrate. The stream is even used as a parade route and festival space. Although the density is much higher in Seoul than in any other of the case studies, this example demonstrates the ability of barriers to become catalysts for re-unification.

Notably, the cities examined in these case studies have widely varying populations, densities and urban fabrics. The urban fabric is formed over time through its own urban process. Some fabrics openly exhibit their scars while others attempt to conceal them. Jane Jacobs makes the case that "frequent streets and short blocks are valuable because of the fabric of intricate cross-use that they permit among the users of a city neighborhood." (Jacobs, 1961) While the cited precedents have widely varying block sizes, the most walkable of those cities are indeed the ones with the noticeably smaller block sizes and higher densities.

"The main function of urban squares is gathering citizens together for various reasons and activities. They have a symbolic meaning of "coexistence". Hence, urban public squares are the essential elements of the city in terms of democracy. Citizens from different social, economic, and cultural backgrounds, age groups, etc. all have equal accessibility to the public spaces. Urban squares are one of these public spaces where individuals and groups learn to respect and tolerate "others". Hence, urban squares are the places where the social interaction and social cohesion occurs." (Memluk, 2013)

Several lessons can be garnered on the efficacy the urban plaza or square as an urban catalyst from the aforementioned case studies. The qualities which were enumerated in each instance can be summarized to the following attributes; a successful urban plaza is to be adaptable, identifiable (provide the area with an image which reflects its identity), have programmed edges, and be accessible (reaching into the surrounding urban fabric).

Catalytic development incorporates concepts of "granularity, incrementalism, walkability, and mixing of uses, scales, and people, and can offer solutions to difficult urban problems while delivering long-term economic returns to both the public and private sectors. It represents an opportunity to do well while doing good." (Leinberger & Loh, 2018).

"Public squares enhance urban livability and provide new anchors to downtown development" - Project for Public Spaces

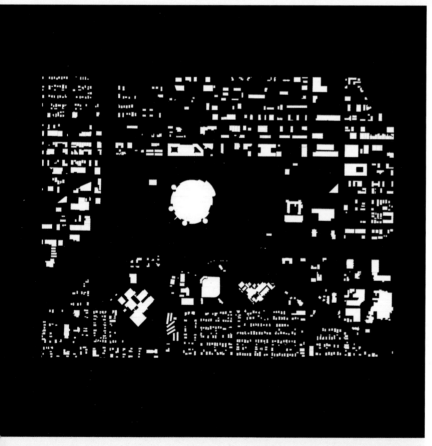

Tropicana Field Site, St Petersburg, FL
Population: 263,255

In light of the place which the Gas Plant neighborhood held within the larger African American community, the site's physical location as a threshold on the edge of starkly divided racial demographics, and its adjacency to downtown St Petersburg, the placement of an urban plaza has the potential to be an asset to both the local community and the city at a larger scale.

Since Straub Park currently serves the community as its public plaza, where the city organizes public events such as First Night for New Year's Eve, the Fourth of July Fireworks and various festivals, the following urban analysis was conducted to serve as a comparative study between Straub Park and the Tropicana Field site.

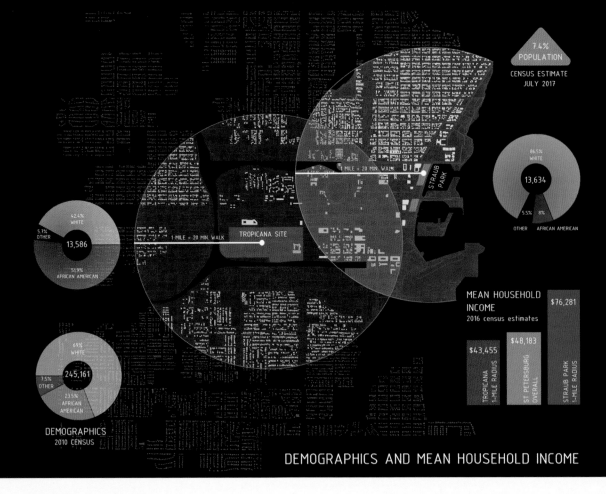

7.4% POPULATION
CENSUS ESTIMATE
JULY 2017

1 MILE = 20 MIN. WALK

STRAUB PARK

TROPICANA SITE

1 MILE = 20 MIN. WALK

5.7% OTHER

42.4% WHITE

13,586

51.9% AFRICAN AMERICAN

86.5% WHITE

13,634

5.5% OTHER   8% AFRICAN AMERICAN

69% WHITE

7.5% OTHER

245,161

23.5% AFRICAN AMERICAN

DEMOGRAPHICS
2010 CENSUS

MEAN HOUSEHOLD INCOME
2016 census estimates

$76,281
STRAUB PARK 1-MILE RADIUS

$48,183
ST PETERSBURG OVERALL

$43,455
TROPICANA 1-MILE RADIUS

DEMOGRAPHICS AND MEAN HOUSEHOLD INCOME

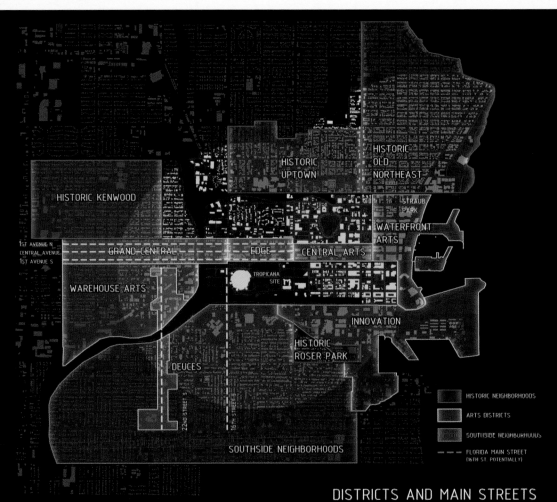

HISTORIC UPTOWN

HISTORIC OLD NORTHEAST

HISTORIC KENWOOD

STRAUB PARK

WATERFRONT ARTS

1ST AVENUE N
CENTRAL AVENUE
1ST AVENUE S

GRAND CENTRAL

EDGE

CENTRAL ARTS

WAREHOUSE ARTS

TROPICANA SITE

INNOVATION

HISTORIC ROSER PARK

DEUCES

22ND STREET S

16TH STREET S

SOUTHSIDE NEIGHBORHOODS

HISTORIC NEIGHBORHOODS
ARTS DISTRICTS
SOUTHSIDE NEIGHBORHOODS
— — — FLORIDA MAIN STREET
(16TH ST POTENTIALLY)

DISTRICTS AND MAIN STREETS

Demographics and Mean Household Income

2010 Census Data and 2016-2017 Census Estimates were used to generate the first graphic to the left. The Demographics and Mean Household Income within a 1-mile radius of Straub Park and Tropicana Field compared to overall St Petersburg demonstrate that the racial demographics within a 1-mile radius of Tropicana field more aptly represent St Petersburg's overall diversity.

Even more striking, is the difference in mean household income within 1-mile radius of Straub Park and overall St Petersburg with a +$28,098 difference while the mean household income differential between Tropicana Field and overall St Petersburg is only -$4,728, keeping in consideration the overlap which exists between the radii of the sampled areas.

The figure-ground underlay shows the residential uses only. The population totals between the two zones are nearly the same with 13,634 in the Straub Park radius and 13,586 in the Tropicana radius. Considering that the Tropicana radius includes 86 acres of developable land, the population density stands to increase significantly due to new development. The census has also provided an estimate of a 7.4% population increase from the 2010 figures by 2020 due to past trends and overall growth as observed across Floridian metropolitan areas.

Districts and Main Streets

The graphic to the left juxtaposes the historic districts, downtown arts districts, and southside St Petersburg. The figure-ground underlay includes residential and non-residential uses. The Deuces was designated as a historic business district and a Florida Main Street in 2001. According to the Florida Division of Historic Resources, a Florida main street program is "a technical assistance program with the goal of revitalizing historic downtowns and encouraging economic development within the context of historic preservation". Four streets in St Petersburg, including historic 22nd St. S., also referred to as the Deuces, have qualified for this designation as shown on the map. 1st Ave N, Central Ave, and 1st Ave S. also carry that designation and there are efforts underway to obtain this designation for 16th St S, which is directly adjacent to the site. Florida Main streets receive funding to revitalize "streets of historic significance with the aim of creating jobs by attracting new industry, improve the area's tax base and preserve the community's historic resources." (Florida Division of Historical Resources).

St Petersburg's Florida Main Streets all exist within a 1-mile radius surrounding the Tropicana site and bring promise of economic growth and potential to benefit the adjacent neighborhoods, as well as the potential development on the site. Also of note, the Tropicana field radius includes southside neighborhoods, the Deuces, Warehouse Arts district, Grand Central District, Edge District, Central Arts District, Innovation District, Historic Roser Park, Historic Kenwood, and Historic Uptown. The Straub Park radius includes Historic Old Northeast, Historic Uptown, Waterfront Arts, Central Arts and Innovation District. The Tropicana radius reaches across a greater variety of districts and can be a pedestrian destination to a wider and more diverse portion of St Petersburg's population.

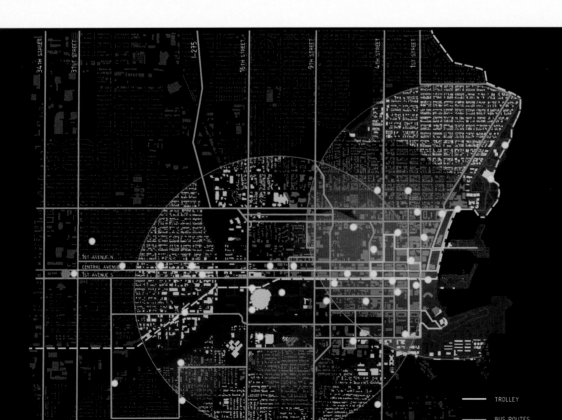

22ND AVENUE N

5TH AVENUE N

1ST AVENUE N
CENTRAL AVENUE
1ST AVENUE S

5TH AVENUE S

18TH AVENUE S

22ND AVENUE S

I-375

STRAUB
PARK

TROPICANA
SITE

I-175

BEACH DRIVE

—— TRAFFIC ARTERIES

● INTERSTATE EXIT

NON-RESIDENTIAL USES AND ACCESS ARTERIES

1ST AVENUE N
CENTRAL AVENUE
1ST AVENUE S

— TROLLEY

BUS ROUTES

Non-Residential Uses and Access Arteries

The figure-ground drawing in the background displays the non-residential uses juxtaposed with the access arteries to highlight the commercial corridors which exist along St Petersburg's major traffic arteries. Although the interstate exits bypass the site and the core of the southside neighborhood, the Tropicana site is clearly more accessible from all directions and capable of accommodating higher traffic densities. Straub Park's location on Downtown's edge inherently restricts accessibility. Larger scale events or even multiple events tend to cause traffic congestion and a shortage of parking.

Public Transit and Walkability

The figure-ground displays all uses because public transit, by design, links residential with non-residential uses. The existing trolley route and bus routes are shown in yellow and green respectively. The Pinellas trail, the successful conversion of the abandoned railroad tracks into a cross-county bicycle path is shown as the dotted blue line along with the blue spots which show the city's bike share locations. The Pinellas Trail notably crosses the Tropicana Field site on its way to the waterfront where the trail has been extended to move northward. The area is well endowed with public transportation options and alternate forms of transit. The most compelling layer on this map is the walkability cloud in pink. Retrieved from the website walkscore.com which provides walkability ratings for cities around the world, the cloud shown on the map is the area of St Petersburg which is considered most walkable. St Petersburg, overall, has a relatively low walk score of 43, because cars are mostly required for effective movement through the city. Downtown and the portions of southside shown have a walkability score of over 70, up to 100 in the heart of downtown, with the Tropicana Field site and the highways as a void in a state of tension between them.

The city has a progressive agenda to expand public transit options and provide transportation alternatives for its residents and as the map illustrates, the systems are in place with much opportunity for growth.

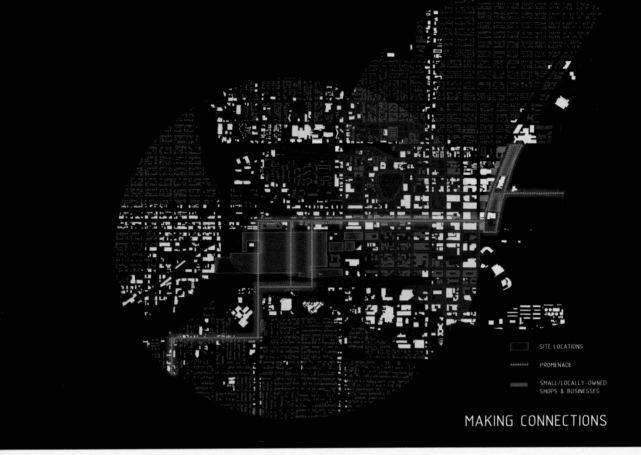

Legend:
SITE LOCATIONS
PROMENADE
SMALL/LOCALLY-OWNED SHOPS & BUSINESSES

37

Making Connections

While the previous graphics have compared and contrasted data and conditions between Straub Park and the Tropicana Field site, the intent, ultimately, is to create connections. The prior data mapping demonstrates the Tropicana Field site's potential at becoming a destination which serves a complementary role to Straub Park. On the map above, the underlay displays all uses with both sites highlighted in green. The sites are no longer contrasted with each other but linked through a promenade lined with St Petersburg's small and locally own ed businesses in pink. The city has, so far, successfully preserved its small business corridors on Beach Drive and Central Avenue and recently passed " the Storefront Conservation Corridor plan, [which] encompasses Beach Drive from Fifth Avenue N to First Avenue S and Central Avenue from First Street to 31st Street" (Moore, 2019) to further preserve the benefits reaped by locals of keeping their money local. The Tropicana site offers a perfect vehicle to connect this Storefront Conservation Corridor Plan area to the existing small business corridors which already exist on the southside on 16h St S and 22nd St S, which, due to funding from the Florida Main Streets program, are poised for growth in the near future.

The importance of the small business in re-establishing the Southside neighborhood's links to Downtown cannot be understated. "High rents, displacement, small businesses being replaced by large chains" (Moskowitz, 2017) are the greatest threats which could impact the southside community if the Tropicana Field site is developed only to maximize profit. The approach needs to be balanced. The area is in need of and will benefit greatly from new development as long as it is programmed to be inclusive. As Rev. Haynes told me, the site needs to incorporate quality affordable housing and quality jobs. As the new development increases the value of the area, the local residents will need to benefit from this increased value, not to be displaced by it. Creating a small business incubator around an urban plaza, which could form a synergy between it and large industry on site would offer a range of employment opportunities within walking distance. These design strategies will only be effective when paired with bold and progressive policies.

When addressing the topic of urban renewal, the issue of gentrification is critical to confront. Although the city of Cincinnati is putting in place policies which will help to deter the population displacement which is typically associated with revitalization efforts, many of the previously mentioned precedent studies have gentrified the areas which they ultimately improved.

As previously exhibited, in relation to the Gas Plant neighborhood, "gentrification is a void in a neighborhood, in a city, in a culture. In that way, gentrification is a trauma, one caused by the influx of massive amounts of capital into a city and the consequent destruction following in its wake." (Moskowitz, 2017) The topic of gentrification can be a controversial topic only due to a possible misunderstanding of the forces involved with the process. Gentrification can only occur in an environment of " deeply rooted inequality; if we were all equal, there could be no gentrifier and no gentrified, no perpetrator or victim." (Moskowitz, 2017) One of the drivers for gentrification is a "political system focused more on the creation and expansion of business opportunity than on the well-being of its citizens" (Moskowitz, 2017). The solution cannot be that, for a neighborhood to undergo economic improvement, its population needs to be replaced. A progressive, balanced, and responsible approach to design must be undertaken to maximize benefit to all the parties involved.

Moving forward with the design of the Tropicana Field Site, it will be of utmost importance to consider strategies which will mitigate the potential harm that the new development could cause to the existing population.

The solution will be to put in place strategies to encourage and allow for local residents to participate and have a stake in the new development, as previously discussed in relation to small business. This end can be achieved by designing the neighborhood to be of mixed income. This strategy is comprised of two main aspects. The neighborhood needs to provide affordable housing side-by-side with market-rate housing and in order to encourage economic self-sufficiency, the neighborhood needs to provide business opportunity. The city could enact a progressive requirement in the masterplan which states that 30% of residential units within each building are required to be affordable housing units, as is a strategy currently implemented in other countries. In the Netherlands, for example, affordability had been decreasing for lower income households in urban settings. The government put in place the new Housing Act 2015, in which "social landlords are required to engage in annual agreements with municipalities and representatives of their tenants on their policy including new construction, investments in sustainability and rent price policy (including rent increases)." (Schilder & Scherpenisse , 2018) This was a movement toward the decentralization of housing policy to allow for municipalities to make decisions which are appropriate for their own housing markets. Much of their affordable housing is handled through housing associations which will often invest in "mixed-income developments with breakdowns such as: 20% low income; 60% middle income; 20% high income. In these developments, high income housing helps pay for the low-income housing to make it a sustainable model for market development. As of 1994, housing associations have been able to continue to build on this model entirely without government funding." (Van Boom, 2018) Although the American system is set-up differently and puts less emphasis on the notion of appropriate affordable housing as a social contract, there is benefit to considering the idea of integrated social housing rather than the proven failures that have resulted from income-segregated neighborhoods or the "ghettoization of different populations" (Van Boom, 2018)

39   "One must always maintain their connection to the past,

and yet ceaselessly pull away from it" - Gaston Bachelard

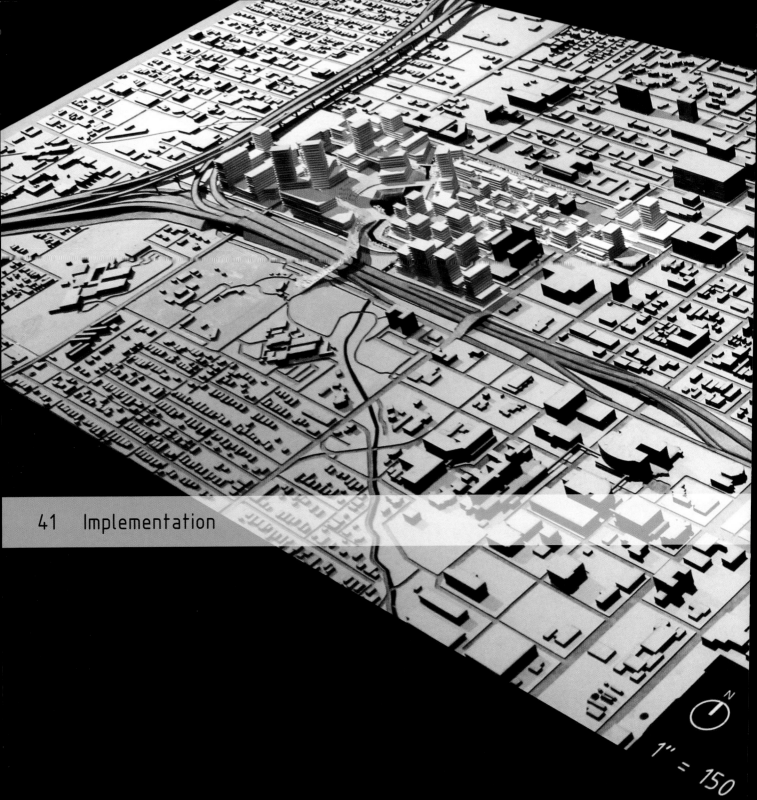

41   Implementation

1" = 150

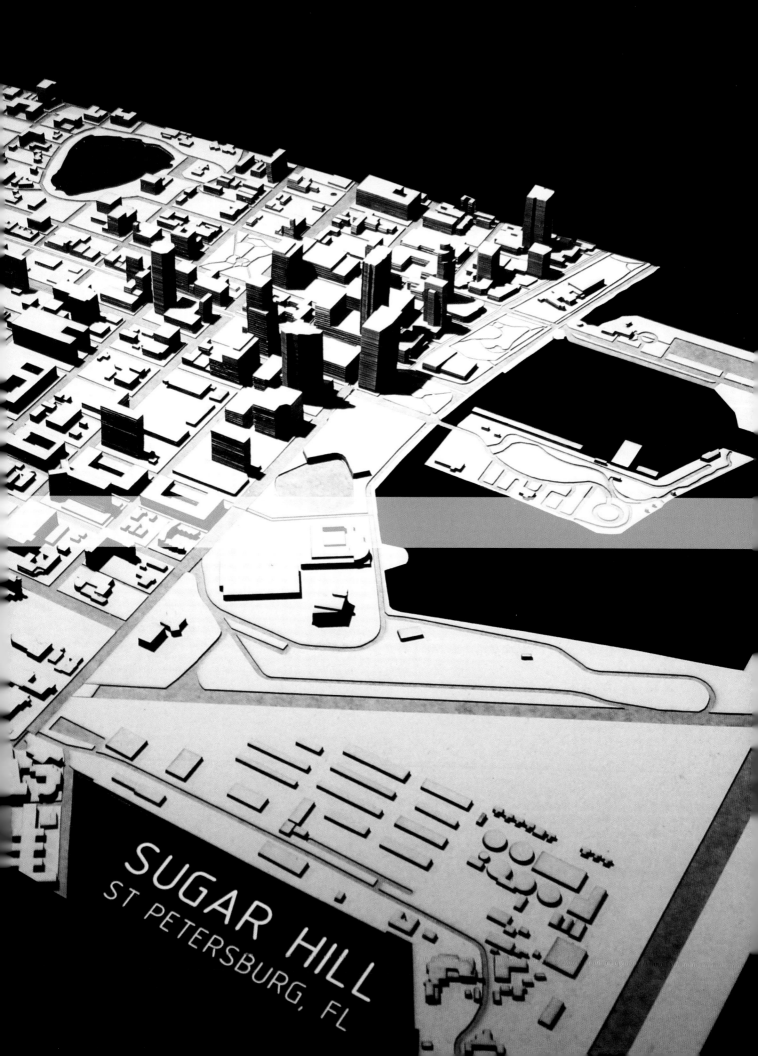

SUGAR HILL
ST PETERSBURG, FL

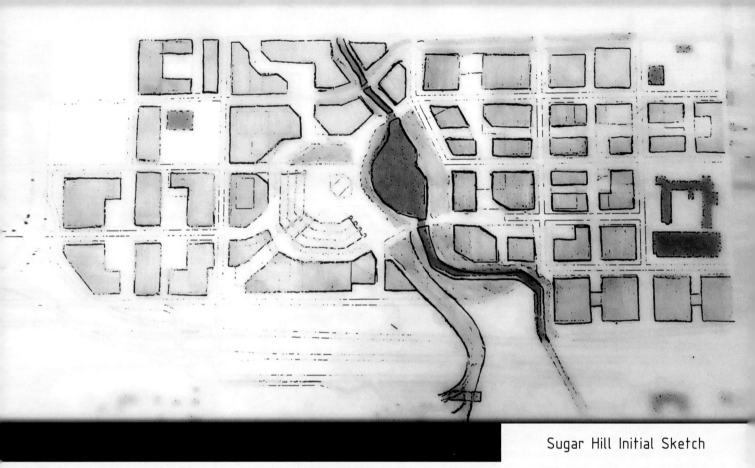

43   Sugar Hill

The first step towards implementation was to rethink the name of the site. Although this thesis does not suggest adopting any specific name, the suggestion is that the site's name should be reconsidered to allow for community input. The neighborhood was initially named Cooper's Quarters until the Gas Plant was established; at which time it was referred to by that name. Bringing back the name of the Gas Plant, I would argue, is merely recalling that the site previously had gas cylinders on it, which polluted the site and were quite unsightly. The gas plant did not positively contribute to the character of the neighborhood, nor does it speak of its prior occupants. The cylinders were there despite the presence of people. The residents gave their sub-neighborhoods other names. While some of the names were tied to the landowners, I have not uncovered the meaning behind "Little Egypt" or "The Hollow", however the meaning behind the name Sugar Hill is easily accessible.

The name Sugar Hill, like the Manhattan Casino, was inspired from New York City's Harlem Renaissance in the 1920s and 30s. Sugar Hill was at the epicenter of the movement and "home to prominent African-American professionals, political leaders, artists, musicians and writers" and "likely named for the sweet life its affluent residents were thought to enjoy in its heyday" (Gregor, 2015).

It is befitting to name this place in a way which speaks of hope, attainment, and success since these values are universally shared.

Fig 22.
Sugar Hill, NY

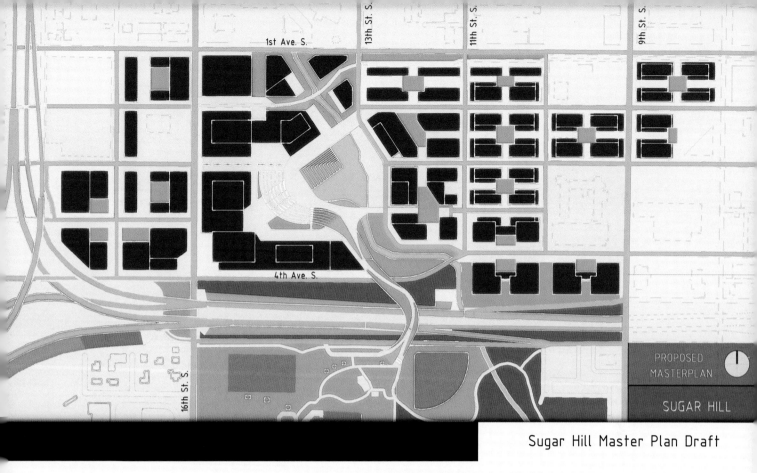

From a design perspective, the city grid needs to be re-introduced onto the site to mend the urban fabric. The first studies of the site, pictured above, establish the basic gestures. The streets are pulled back into the site from the existing grid. A reservoir has been created in the heart of the site from Booker Creek to celebrate the presence of water on the site. "Water surfaces within a square provide habitat for living organisms. Existence of green areas within a public square also helps to improve air quality, lessen surface water runoff, reduce noise levels and screen unwanted or undesirable views, and reduce negative effects of urban heat islands." (Memluk, 2013) Cleaning up the creek and creating a water reservoir also allows for the site's occupants and visitors to touch the water. St Petersburg is known for its sandy beaches, and its downtown waterfront where the public realm stops abruptly at the edge of the water. St Petersburg's residents and visitors can either go to the beach to touch the water and get sandy or go downtown to look at it. Could there be something in between? Could the creation of an Urban Beach, where one could take a lunch break from work and get their feet wet without getting sand on their suit, add another dimension to St Petersburg's appeal? St Petersburg has 20 lakes open for shoreline fishing, yet these are inadvisable for public swimming due to the presence of alligators. The "messy" nature of the creek can be removed by designing a constructed water feature as a part of the urban beach adjacent to the urban plaza, which allows for a controlled interaction with water in the spirit of Crown Fountain in Millennium Park, Chicago. The site is effectively divided in half by the creek and its reservoir. The east side of the creek is fully reintegrated into the existing downtown street network. The blocks are fragmented and breathable, allowing for the creation of interior semi-private courtyards. The portion to the west of the creek up to 16th St. S, between 1st Ave. S. and 4th Ave. S. is the Urban beach, which is a Pedestrian only space. Its axis shifts approximately 30 degrees to align with Booker Creek and also as a gesture reaching in the direction of the southwestern exodus of the population in the 1980s, designed as a gesture to re-invite the population in. 13th St S. breaks the rhythm of the grid and follows the direction of the creek, creating a street side retail edge condition for the Urban Beach, mirroring Beach Drive as a street-side retail edge to Straub Park. This street is also the only one from which the Urban Beach can be fully viewed from a vehicle.

Movement Sketch

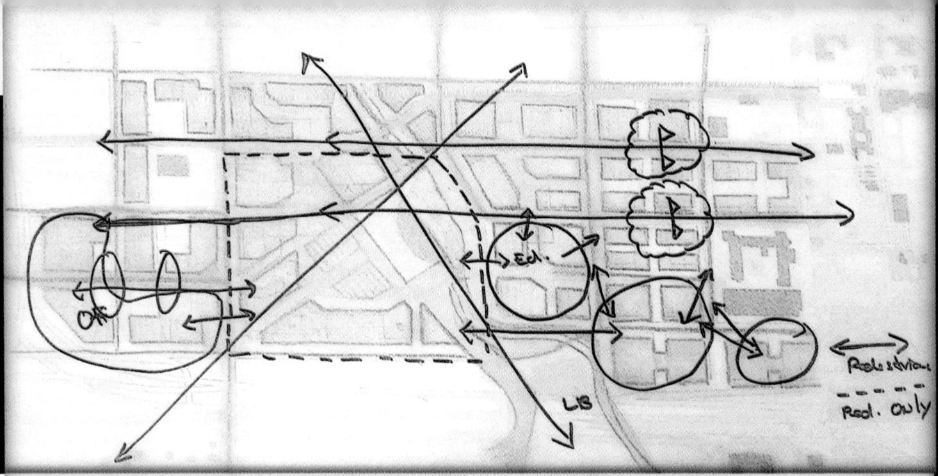

Program Sketch

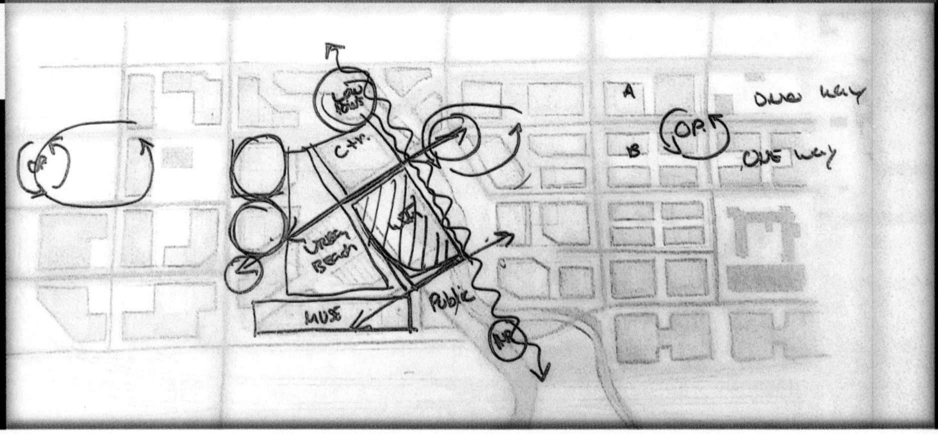

The Urban Beach feature is the nucleus of the site. The act of mending the urban fabric culminates in the urban plaza, which is a gesture of reunification, a place to bring the citizenry together also intended to act as an economic catalyst for the area. The east-west connections are established through 1st Ave s., 2nd Ave s., 3rd Ave. s., 4th Ave. s. as well as the Pinellas Trail. 13th St. s. and 12th St. s. provide northern connections to central avenue and beyond. Central Ave.'s walkability currently fades past 13th St. This proposal offers to extend Central Ave's successful pedestrian-friendly and small storefront model southward and connect it to southside's re-emerging business district. The north-south connection is established through 16th St. s. and 9th St. s. This connection is more challenging due to the physical barrier imposed by the highway. The land bridge acts as a physical connection between the urban plaza, Campbell Park as well as the skate park creating a pedestrian and bicycling connection and an invitation for southside's residents to re-engage.

The Urban Beach's purpose is to extend downtown's public realm towards the center of the city and connect it with its surrounding residential neighborhoods. Connectivity is an essential consideration because of past efforts at division. The Urban Beach's "octopus", pictured right, was designed to maximize pedestrian connections. For these connections to be used and produce intensity "the district, and indeed as many of its internal parts as possible, must serve more than one primary function..." (Jacobs, 1961). With connectivity and flexibility as principle features, the site's mixed-use program needs to be established which will bring people in for many different purposes to activate it.

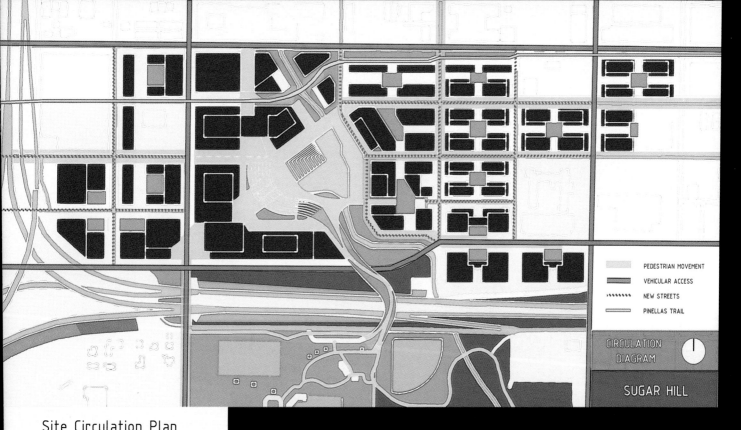

Site Circulation Plan

PEDESTRIAN MOVEMENT
VEHICULAR ACCESS
NEW STREETS
PINELLAS TRAIL

CIRCULATION
DIAGRAM

SUGAR HILL

Octopus

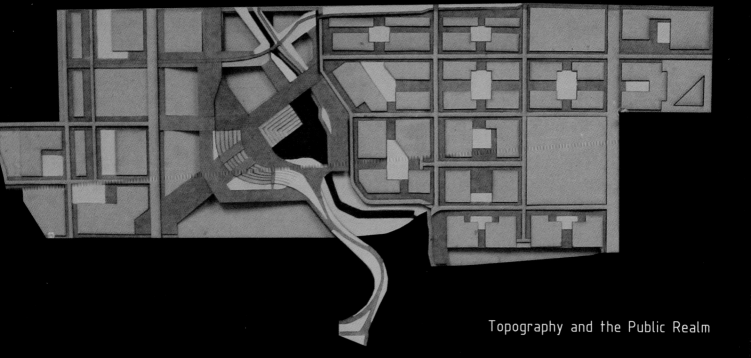

The first study model was created to explore the public realm and with less of a focus on the buildings, since their design, in this proposal, is concerned with their ability to shape the plenum of the public realm and their program content. In the study model pictured above and right, the topography of the site was examined along with the semi-private interior block courtyards and their potential to add a dimension of community at a smaller scale, in between the residents of a block. Depending on the design of each architect which tackles a block, the interior courtyards could contain community gardens, playgrounds, open hard surfaces or gardens, such as the one at the Carter G. Woodson Museum of African American History.

The delineation between the public and private realm must be clearly defined, however, the interior courtyard space offers the opportunity for nodes of activity along the promenade, whether they are related to the residential, office or retail activities programmed on each block. The block is explored further later. The intent is to keep St Petersburg's city promenade beautiful in the spirit of the City Beautiful movement upon which the city was founded and to offer an added element to the choreography of the "sidewalk ballet" (Jacobs, 1961).

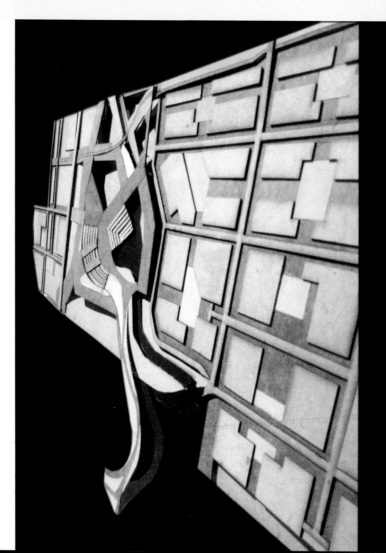

Massing Study

The Massing of the site was another important element to determine in the formation of the public realm. The building facades form the plenum of space of the public realm and give the street its spatial character. The building footprints were first established to design the two-dimensional web of movement around the neighborhood. Tampa Bay's tallest building to date is The One, located in downtown St Petersburg, rising at 41 stories and 450 ft. The intent of the development on this site is not to compete with downtown's waterfront district, but rather to compliment it. The buildings around the Urban Beach are designed to be the tallest on the site to clearly define the edge of the public plaza, in the manner that Piazza del Campo does. These tall, iconic, buildings will become a visual landmark for pedestrians approaching the site from all directions and create a sense of destination. The city's effort at unity has the potential to be as grand as its past efforts at disunity. Tall office buildings are placed along the highway as a barrier shielding the residential core from this unpleasant edge. To the east of the site, the super-block model which is currently being employed in the redesign of the city's downtown blocks is gradually fragmented into the core of the residential mixed-use neighborhood.

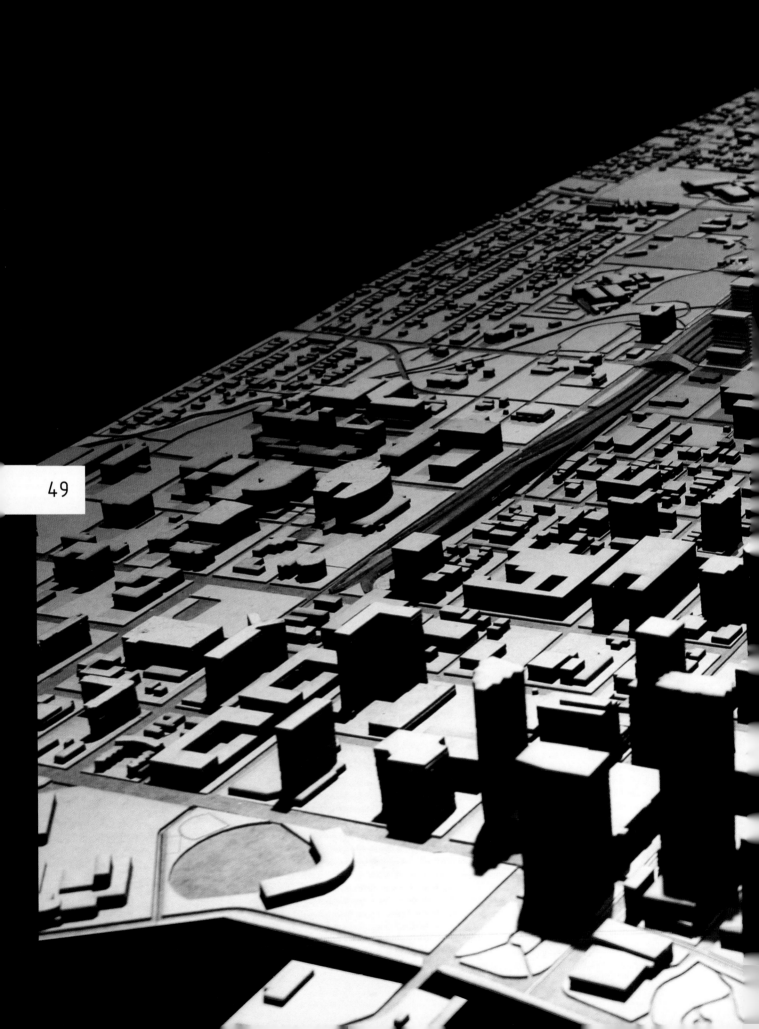

49

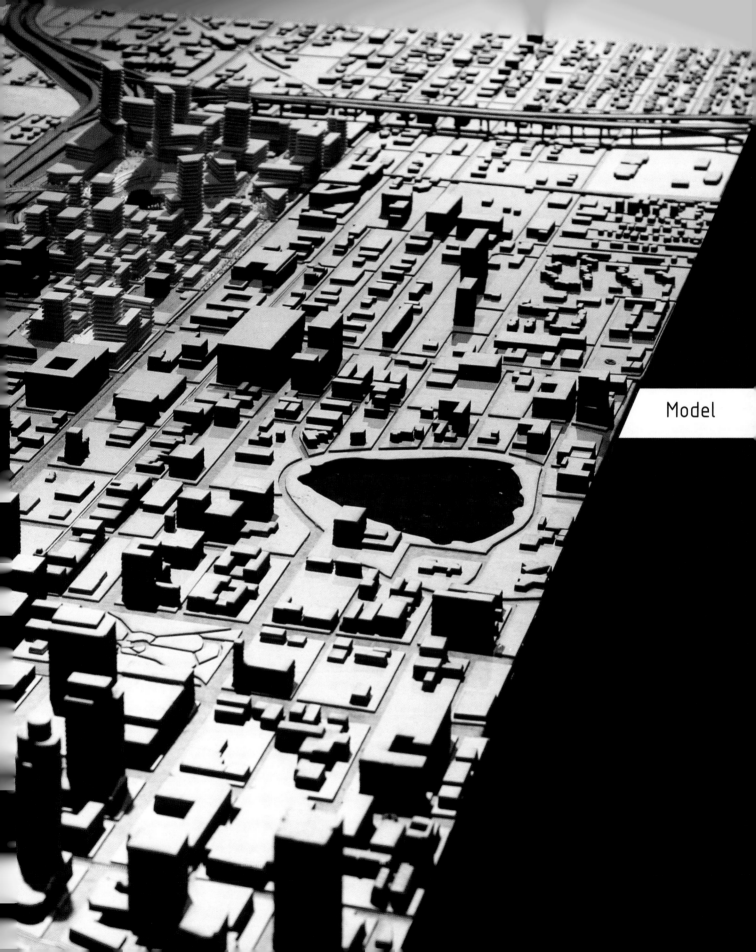

Model

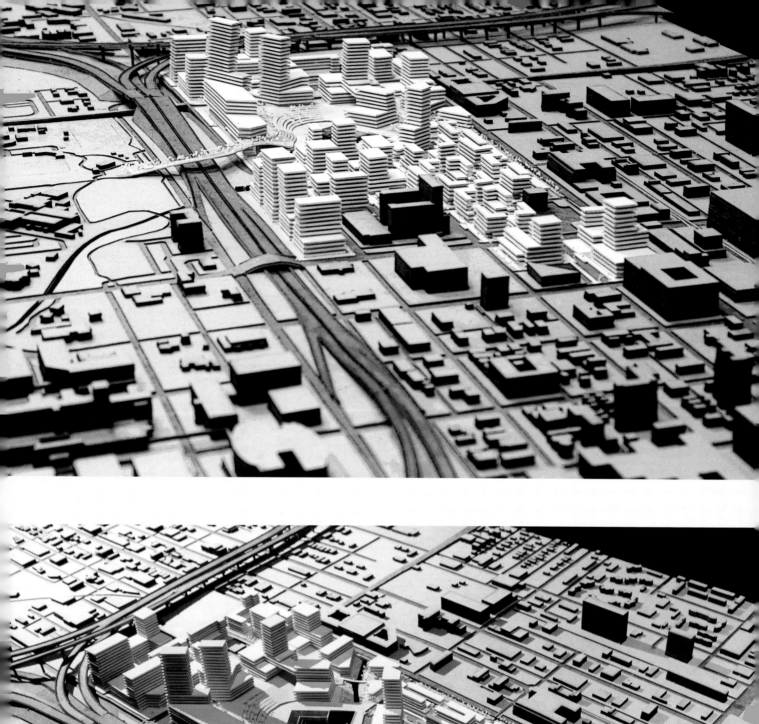

55

57

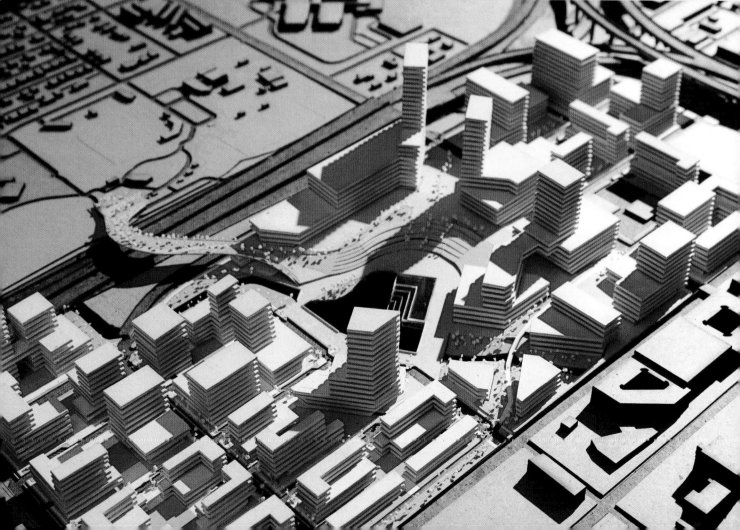

59

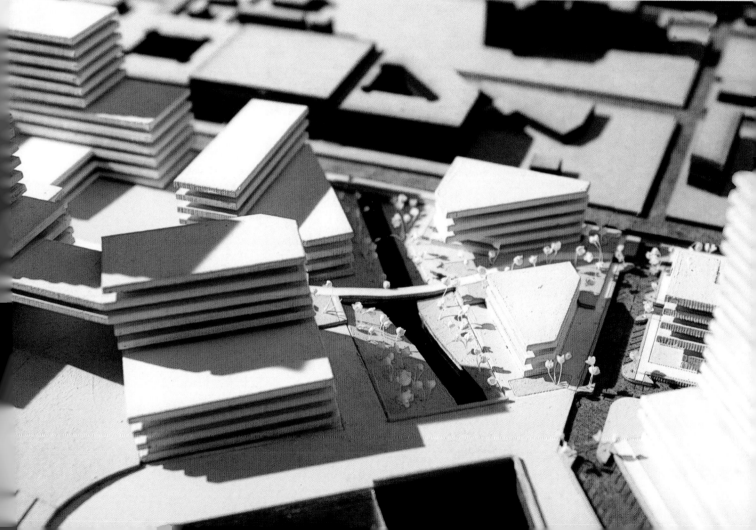

63

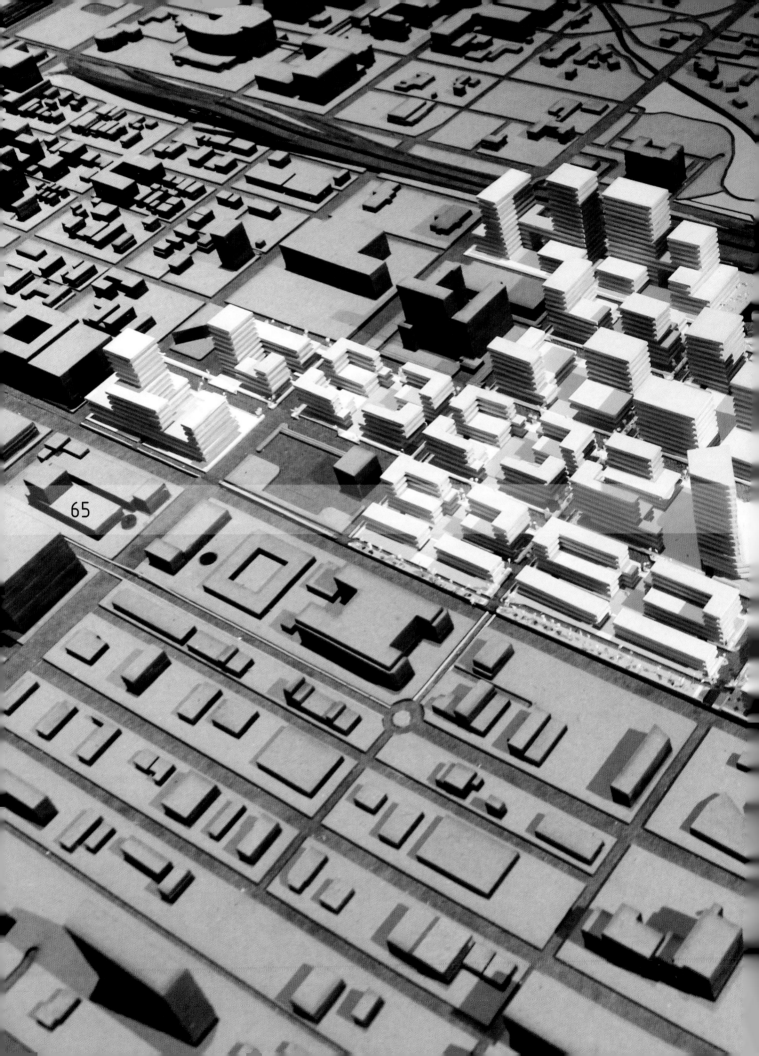

65

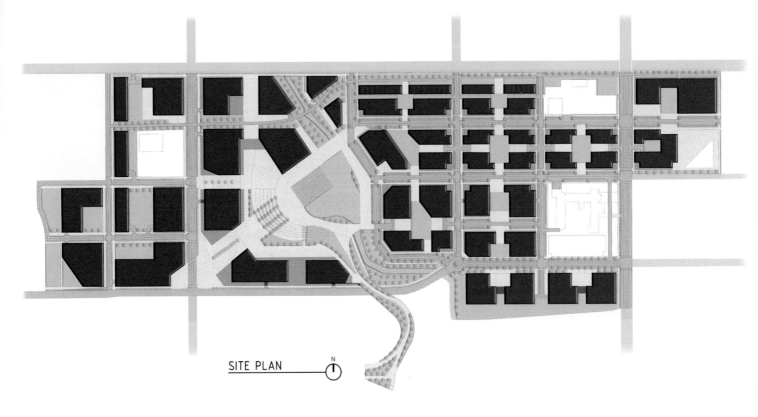

SITE PLAN   N

67   Program

The study of the physical fabric of the city reveals the inefficient use of surface parking lots actively being replaced by super-blocks with parking integrated into buildings. This proposal includes off-street parking on the retail streets, 2nd Ave. s., 3rd Ave. s. and 13th St S., keeping in character with Beach Dr. and Central Ave. The remainder of the parking is to be nestled within the buildings. In comparison to the approximately 6,000 spaces offered by the site currently, this proposal offers, 615 off-street parking spaces and enough square footage to accommodate 7,750 parking spaces within the buildings, which would serve residents, patrons and visitors to the site. The site information to the right details the proposed area calculations and the proposed density. As previously mentioned, programming is essential to the success of the site, and is detailed on the axonometric to the right. The office buildings were designed to line the highway, shielding the residential core and public realm from some of the noise pollution generated from the highway as well as its unsightly view. Parking garages line the highway with the office spaces placed above. These large buildings have the capability of hosting large corporations that may want to relocate to St Petersburg. The office retail buildings offer a step down in density from the office-only buildings and are integrated into the residential mixed-use fabric which defines the site's character with the presence of ground floor retail, ideally comprised of locally owned small business retail tenants. Most of the buildings on the site belong to the office-retail-residential category. The importance of this typology, iterated in different scales on the site, contributes to the creation of a dynamic sidewalk ballet as described by Jane Jacobs in The Death and Life of Great American Cities. The character of the sidewalk ballet cannot be specifically prescribed yet designers can provide its framework. The synergy created by the office-retail-residential use guarantees eyes on the street and usage at all times of day leading to an increased sense of community and perception of safety. The creation of neighborhoods which provide work opportunity for its residents increase their walkability and disincentivizes the overuse of cars. Educational and civic uses are placed on the edge of the creek and the convention center/hotel is located on the edge of the Urban Beach which will act as an intense activator of the public plaza. An option of residential only buildings in the form of row houses, lining the Pinellas Trail, and apartment buildings are offered as an alternative to the mixed-use residential typology.

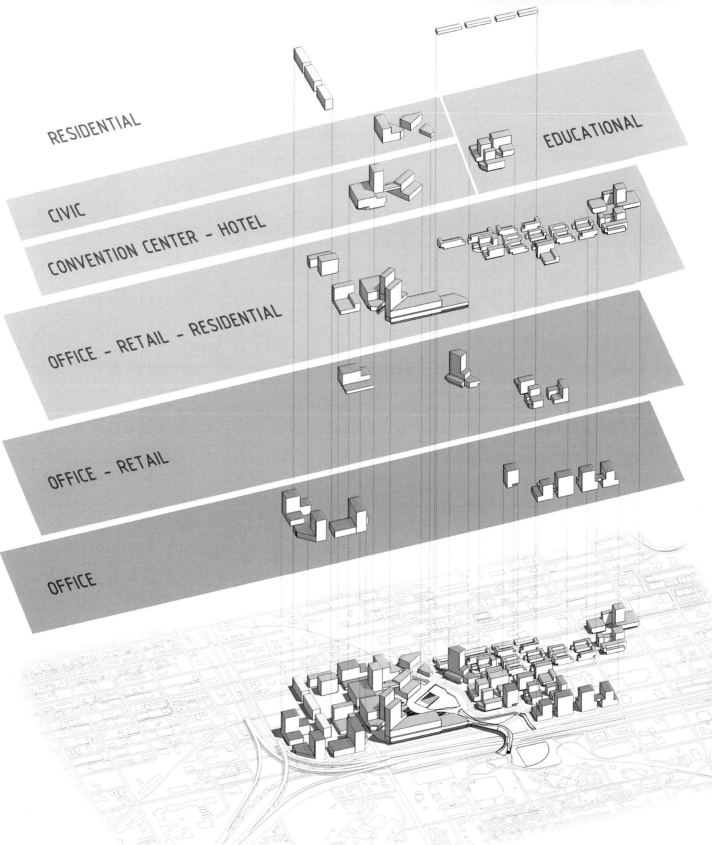

RESIDENTIAL

EDUCATIONAL

CIVIC

CONVENTION CENTER – HOTEL

OFFICE – RETAIL – RESIDENTIAL

OFFICE – RETAIL

OFFICE

Existing Conditions:

Land area:	86 acres
	3,750,000 sq.ft.
Parking: Approx.	6000 spaces
Stadium Area:	1,100,000 sq. ft.

Proposed Design:

Off-Street Parking:	615 spaces	Civic Use:	400,000 sq.ft.
Parking Garage Spaces:	7,750 spaces	Educational Use:	350,000 sq.ft.
Residential Use:	1,610,000 sq.ft.		
	1610 units		
	19 units/acre	Gross Built Area:	6,510,000 sq.ft
30% Affordable Housing:	483 units	FAR:	1.8
Retail Use:	400,000 sq.ft.		
Office Use:	3,000,000 sq.ft.		

SITE INFORMATION

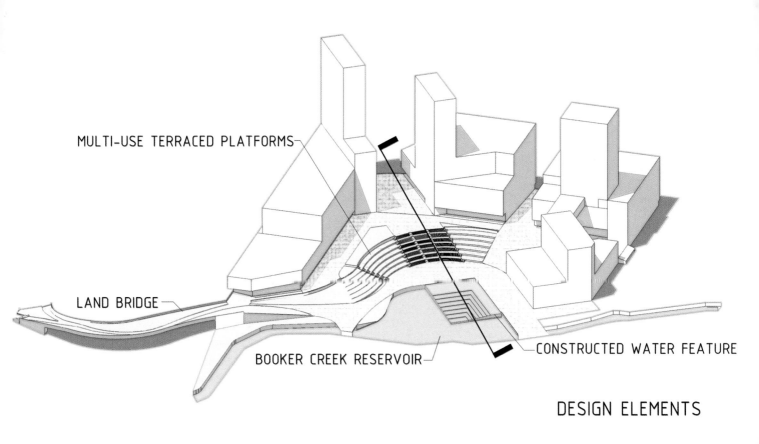

MULTI-USE TERRACED PLATFORMS

LAND BRIDGE

BOOKER CREEK RESERVOIR

CONSTRUCTED WATER FEATURE

DESIGN ELEMENTS

69   Urban Beach

RESIDENTIAL

HOTEL

OFFICE

RETAIL

CONVENTION CTR

PARKING

USE SECTION

Urban Beach is programmed with several design elements which will contribute to its success as an urban plaza and connection node between southside St Petersburg and downtown. Urban Beach begins with the land bridge which acts as a threshold between Campbell Park and the urban plaza space. The land bridge is a physical patch over the highway separating southside from downtown. It is a means by which pedestrians rise above the highway barrier and descend onto the plaza area enjoying an elevated view of the neighborhood. It is not just a bridge, such as can currently be found on the site, which is seldom used. It is a symbolic procession onto the site, an invitation. The path splits where the bridge lands, one towards the water and the other towards the building edges. The land bridge transitions into the multi-use terraced platforms, 25 ft in width, which can serve as amphitheater seating for large scale events, or even platforms upon which to accommodate pop up markets, art shows, or school picnics (given the adjacency of the site to two schools). The platforms are interrupted by grand stairs, aligning with the southwestern axis and the constructed water feature. The water feature is comprised of gently sloped terraced concrete platforms submerged in filtered creek and rainwater, running back off into the Booker Creek Reservoir. The sound of water movement improves the soundscape quality in an urban setting (Yang & Kang, 2005). Water evokes the fluidity of time and space. The connection to the water is a connection to the memory of this place.

"In observation studies of modern plaza use; sitting, standing, walking and their combinations with eating, reading, watching and listening account for more than 90% of use" (Marcus & Francis, 1997).

An urban plaza needs to provide basic programming features but also retain flexibility. The edge of the Urban Beach is lined with retail with enough footprint to allow for a grocery store to occupy either the ground level or 2nd floor. There is no grocery store in the entire southside portion on the map which depicted the African American density of over 80%. Two grocery stores have come and gone on 22nd St S and 18th Ave. S. Rev. Haynes indicated to me that the grocery stores didn't generate the revenue that they were anticipating because the neighborhood's residents don't have access to good paying jobs to generate the income to support the stores.

By strengthening the social fabric, providing economic opportunity, and boosting the well-being of citizens, public space can make limited resources go further and enrich the community both socially and financially - Project for Public Spaces

This purpose must be served by the site. It needs to be a place of opportunity, which provides someone who has a dream with a platform to realize that dream. Inviting, not subsidizing, large industry to occupy the office buildings on-site provides a clientele for the locally owned businesses at the ground level, if their right to be there is preserved. I would argue that the 3 Starbucks coffee shops in downtown St Petersburg serve their purpose, yet locally owned coffee shops and restaurants on the plaza would offer more of St Pete's "sunshine city" character that is well loved by its citizenry and has been transforming it into a destination. The plaza could highlight and celebrate St Petersburg's local flavor rather than exhibit a commercial display of national chains. The convention center/hotel as a building typology has the potential to bring thousands of patrons to the site, some of whom have never been to St Petersburg, and the Urban Beach would be their first pedestrian exposure to the city. Designing small storefront spaces, at the ground level, allows for greater affordability especially for startup businesses. The upper levels could include an array of office sizes and typologies, such as business cooperatives, as suggested by Rev. Haynes, which would allow for start-up entrepreneurs to have access to office amenities in a place that otherwise would be unaffordable for many. The synergy between the different uses, pictured left would provide the city plaza with liveliness throughout the day and into the night. Restaurants and bars will maintain the level of energy until later and the presence of residential units also places eyes and ears on the plaza at all times. The residential units on the plaza are another important aspect of the urban beach as an economic catalyst. These are likely to be overpriced condos, if left unregulated. St Petersburg could lead the way in avoiding the undesirable outcomes of urban renewal, by rethinking affordable housing. Since the plaza is meant to be a unifier of people from different backgrounds and socio-economic statuses, the residents of the site should reflect the same diversity. By requiring developers to include a certain percentage of affordable housing, and middle-income housing units, opportunity is extended to a larger portion of the population to live and thrive in a place which offers opportunity for growth. The same amenities should not be afforded to all units as it would cause resentment among the residents paying a higher price. Price can be determined in terms of views, materials used in interior construction, amenities offered within the units, balconies, and so on... With the proper design and regulations in place, Urban Beach has the potential to benefit the developers and, more importantly, the community which it serves.

Scan to view video

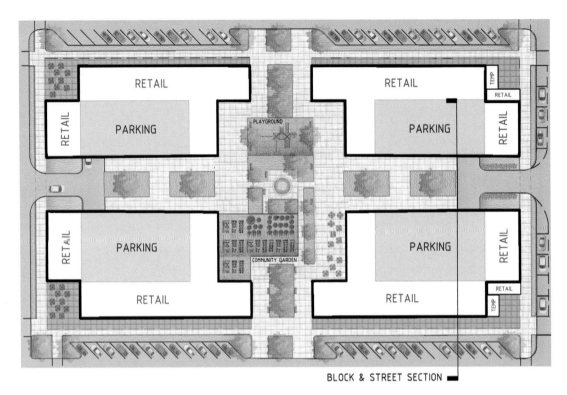

TYPICAL MIXED-INCOME BLOCK PLAN

RETAIL · RETAIL · PARKING · RETAIL · PLAYGROUND · TEMP RETAIL · RETAIL · PARKING · COMMUNITY GARDEN · RETAIL · TEMP · RETAIL

BLOCK & STREET SECTION

81 The Mixed-Income Block

"Two parents, to say nothing of one, cannot possibly satisfy all the needs of a family-household. A community is needed as well, for raising children, and also to keep adults reasonably sane and cheerful. A community is a complex organism with complicated resources that grow gradually and organically." (Jacobs, 2004)

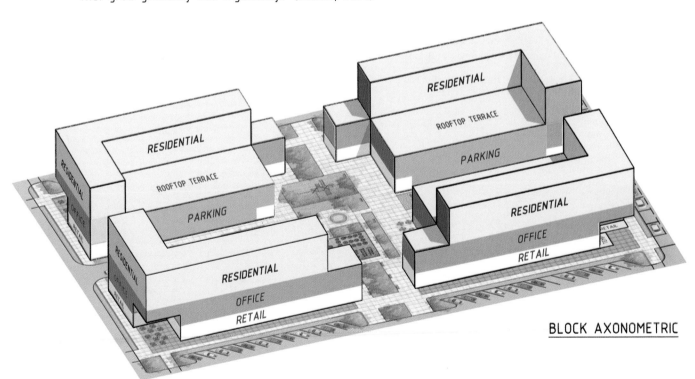

BLOCK AXONOMETRIC

The mixed-income block is another aspect of the site design which was explored. The block was designed as a typology and does not aim to provide a specific building form. The rectangular masses of the buildings were carved into to allow for the following block features to occur. The buildings are composed of retail on the ground level, offices on the 2nd and 3rd level, and residential on the top 3 levels, with parking nestled within the building. The concept of the back alley has been re-imagined, leading to an inner courtyard. The "alley" allows for vehicular access into the buildings and pedestrian access to the courtyard, which can be made semi-private or fully private. These inner courtyards can contain a water feature, playground, garden, exterior workspace for offices, courtyard restaurant seating, or an outdoor area for children to learn to ride bikes in safety. These court spaces can be programmed to suit the needs of the residents and occupants of the site. The rooftop terraces above the parking garages can be used as community gardens, event spaces or rooftop pools. These spaces within the blocks offer a smaller scaled place of connection for communities on the block level. The proposed square footage for the block shown to the left allows for approximately 120 living units. If 30% of these are affordable housing units, each block could provide living accommodations for 36 families. The community space would be available for use by all these families and foster a bond of community between residents and visitors from diverse socio-economic backgrounds. A special emphasis was placed on street corners as well. The block corners are a place of intersection for divergent paths. The building footprint retreats at the corner to allow for outdoor retail activity. Whether it be restaurant seating or temporary retail space which can be rented out on a daily or weekly basis. These temporary spaces "provide opportunity for people at the lower end of the economic spectrum, allowing entrepreneurs....to sustain themselves and their families with a minimum of capital investment." (Project for Public Spaces, 2012) This feature of the block allows for an element of surprise in the sidewalk ballet, introducing the occupants of the block to something new and allowing for the merchant(s) to eventually graduate to a permanent location on site, if their venture successfully builds a clientele and generates enough revenue. The temporary spaces need not conflict with the permanent retail tenants and can assist in bringing increased foot traffic to their sidewalk.

Within the larger neighborhoods, smaller, close-knit residential groupings existed, often identified as "courts" or "quarters".
(Peck & Wilson, 2008)

As demonstrated in the street section below, the building footprint retreats to allow the floors above to act as a canopy, a protection from the sun or the heavy rains which can arrive unexpectedly in the summer months. In Florida, generally, the pedestrian experience tends to be an afterthought, as much of the infrastructure is designed to facilitate vehicular movement. Simply retreating the building footprint increases the sidewalk width, increases pedestrian safety, and provides sorely needed shelter on a summer day. Although the city experiences an influx of visitors during the cooler season, the summer promenade can be made more appealing to permanent residents by providing building-integrated shelter from the elements. The inclusion of a landscape buffer, shade-bearing trees, and off-street parking further separates the pedestrian promenade from moving traffic, which increases its quality. With these features implemented at the scale of the block and ultimately the street, the site will no longer exist as an impediment to pedestrian movement but rather as a catalyst for it.

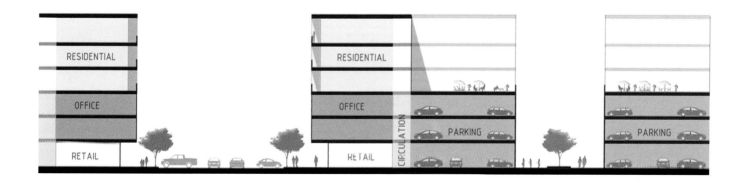

BLOCK & STREET SECTION

83   "A living culture is forever changing, without losing itself as a framework and context of change.

The reconstruction of a culture is not the same as its restoration." (Jacobs, 2004)

85 Conclusion

The intent of this proposal is to call for the site to be designed as an ecosystem which benefits its surrounding communities, the city, and its investors - financially and socially. Examining the site's history is a critical step towards developing relevant and progressive strategies for inclusivity. The consequences of St Petersburg's urban renewal efforts, despite any of its intentions, have resulted in population displacement and economic suffering for populations that have been historically marginalized and often occupied these areas for generations.

Our "ideals of urban identity, citizenship and belonging" (Harvey, 2003) need to be re-examined, as a broader society, to identify how to construct our environments responsibly. A study of this history reveals that the city, in the past, exhibited consistent disregard towards the health and vitality of its African American community as recently as the 1980s. The persistent attempts at erasure and disempowerment of this community and its culture over time must be followed with equally persistent efforts toward inclusivity and empowerment.

The Urban Beach concept brings downtown intensity into the heart of St Petersburg. It is a connective tissue, placed upon the urban fabric. The city's heart beats in its core, where the majority of its residents reside. Its edges are beautiful and properly celebrated. Yet the addition of a public plaza in the heart of the city, to be a small business incubator, powered by its residents and, in part, by the presence of large industry, can create a successful synergy which can bring economic benefit to surrounding communities. The implementation of progressive policies is integral to the success of the discussed design features aimed at elevating the area. The urban plaza is the city's public living room, where people from different walks of life can live, work, play, and connect. Its location on the threshold of the city's history, culture and memory is a warranted gesture of unity.

Although two- and three-dimensional studies of the built environment can inform the future morphology of the site and the design of its components, these are all merely a framework which its people will infill with their stories. Designers and city officials will determine the quality of that framework and the types of stories which it will invite and support, yet the voices of its citizens will ultimately recount the city's story.

Mrs. Rosalie Peck wondered in her last chapter, "Where have all the Mangoes gone?"

"Everywhere were wonderful fruit-bearing trees that seemed to belong to no one and to everyone. It was a time when south-side children enjoyed access to an endless abundance of hunger-chasing, gut-filling, taste-bud satisfying fruit from trees of unlimited kindness. Merciful shade-bearing trees sagged heavy with guavas, avocados, oranges, grapefruit, tangerines and lemons, always present for the picking...

Positive role models of old were recalled as being as plentiful as fruit-bearing trees. Revered in memory are parents, relatives, principals, teachers, coaches, preachers, friends, neighbors, professionals in multiple fields and ordinary people doing extraordinary things...

"Do not go where the path may lead, go instead where there is no path and leave a trail" ....

St Petersburg today is nearly bereft of mangoes and other cherished fruit trees from neighborhood yards, but the city is still wealthy with a continuing supply of the soul-sustaining fruit of the human spirit." (Peck & Wilson, 2008)

87   Appendix A - List of Figures

Fig. 1. Cover of St Petersburg's Historic African American Neighborhoods
Peck R, Wilson J. (2008) St. Petersburg's historic African American neighborhoods. Charleston, SC: History Press; 2008.

Fig. 2. Cover of St Petersburg's Historic 22nd Street South
Peck R, Wilson J. (2006) St. Petersburg's Historic 22nd Street South. Charleston, SC: History Press.

Fig. 3. Pinellas County, FL – St Petersburg Highlighted
Arkyan [CC BY-SA 3.0 (http://creativecommons.org/licenses/by-sa/3.0/)] https://upload.wikimedia.org/wikipedia/commons/2/24/Pinellas_County_Florida_Incorporated_and_Unincorporated_areas_St._Petersburg_Highlighted.svg

Fig. 4. Florida Suncoast Done under construction - 1988
Walker M., November 24, 1986, "Stadium Ground Broken". Boca Raton News. Pp 6C.

Fig. 5. The Manhattan Casino
Moore, W.A, November 20th, 2017, St Petersburg Council okays restaurant deal for Manhattan Casino, Tampa Bay Times.

Fig. 6. The Carter G. Woodson Museum of African American History
http://www.woodsonmuseum.org/

Fig. 14. Straub Park, St Petersburg
https://stpeterising.com/

Fig. 15. Piazza del Campo, Siena Italy
https://www.discovertuscany.com/siena/piazza-del-campo.html

Fig. 16. Portsmouth Square
https://www.sfgate.com/bayarea/article/Changes-could-be-in-store-Portsmouth-Square-11106856.php https://scotthessphoto.typepad.com/scott_hess_photography/2010/08/index.html https://www.pps.org/places/portsmouth-square

Fig. 17. Campus Martius
http://downtowndetroitparks.com/parks/Campus-Martius https://www.pps.org/places/campus-martius

Fig. 18. Market Square
https://www.pps.org/projects/pittsburgh-market-square http://www.goodfoodpittsburgh.com/the-good-food-agenda-this-weekends-best-food-events-0614/

Fig. 19. Discovery Green
https://www.discoverygreen.com/jones-lawn https://www.pps.org/projects/houstonpark

Fig. 7. Children Plaiting the Maypole in St Petersburg
Plaiting of the Maypole, September 18th, 2014, the Weekly Challenger. http://theweeklychallenger.com/plaiting-of-the-maypole/

Fig. 8. Jon Wilson and Rosalie Peck
Peck R, Wilson J. (2008) St. Petersburg's historic African American neighborhoods. Charleston, SC: History Press; 2008.

Fig. 9. The Orange Belt Railway
Hensley, D., April 2011, History of the Orange Line, Trains Magazine. http://trn.trains.com/railroads/ask-trains/2011/04/history-of-the-orange-line

Fig. 10. St Petersburg, FL, 1947
https://www.mapsofthepast.com/st-petersburg-florida-topographic-us-army-1947.html

Fig. 11. Lakeview Market
http://hdrbodegaphoto.com/2013/12/lakeside-grocery-st-petersburg-fl/

Fig. 12. Proposed Negro Segregation Project, 1935
St Petersburg Times, December 19th, 1935

Fig. 13. Maps tracing concentrations of growth of St Petersburg's African American communities 1920-1951
Peck R, Wilson J. (2008) St. Petersburg's historic African American neighborhoods. Charleston, SC: History Press; 2008. p.30

Fig. 20. Washington Square Park
https://www.bizjournals.com/cincinnati/morning_call/2014/10/this-cincinnati-park-is-among-the-5-best-in-the-u.html https://cincinnatiusa.com/things-to-do/attractions/washington-park

Fig. 21. Cheonoggyecheon Stream Park
https://greatruns.com/seoul-cheonggyecheon-stream/ https://preparetravelplans.com/cheonggyecheon-stream-guide

Fig. 22. Sugar Hill, NY
https://www.elegran.com/blog/2013/07/in-the-heart-of-harlems-renaissance-sugar-hill

Circular Area Profiles   Missouri Census Data Center

Circular Area Profiles (CAPS) — 2010

Using data from Summary File 1, 2010 Census

Request details:

- Center point name: **straub park, st petersburg**
- Latitude **27.775458**
- Longitude **-82.631460**
- Selected radii: **1**

[CSV file of aggregated data]

1-mile radius of specified point (straub park, st petersburg)

Subject	Number	Percent
1. Total Population Trends, Etc.		
Universe: Total Population		
Total Population	13,634	
Total Population 2000	13,599	
Change in Population 2000-2010	35	0.3
Males	6,898	50.6
Females	6,736	49.4
Population Density	6129	
Land Area Sq. Miles	2	
2. Age		
Universe: Population		
Under 5 Years	331	2.4
Age 5 to 9 Years	339	2.5
10 to 14 Years	301	2.2
15 to 17 Years	174	1.3
18 to 19 Years	406	3.0
20 to 24 Years	976	7.2
25 to 34 Years	2,236	16.4
35 to 44 Years	1,821	13.4
45 to 54 Years	2,154	15.8
55 to 59 Years	1,009	7.4
Age 60 to 64 Years	1,052	7.7
65 to 74 Years	1,476	10.8

Subject	Number	Percent
75 to 84 Years	840	6.2
85 Years and Over	519	3.8
Median Age	46.6	
Age 0 to 17	1,145	8.4
18 to 24 Years	1,382	10.1
25 to 44 Years	4,057	29.8
45 to 64 Years	4,215	30.9
62 Years and Over	3,443	25.3
65 Years and Over	2,835	20.8
3. Race		
Universe: Population		
One Race	13,350	97.9
White	11,787	86.5
Black or African American	1,088	8.0
American Indian and Alaska Native	75	0.6
Asian	238	1.7
Native Hawaiian and Other Pacific Islander	6	0.0
Some Other Race	156	1.1
Multi Race - Persons reporting more than one race	284	2.1
4. Hispanic or Latino and Race		
Universe: Hispanic or Latino Population		
Hispanic or Latino (of any race)	793	5.8
Mexican	NA	
Puerto Rican	NA	
Cuban	NA	
Other Hispanic or Latino	NA	
Not Hispanic or Latino	12,841	94.2
White Alone Not Hispanic	11,222	82.3
5. Relationship of Persons in Households		
Universe: Persons in Households		
Total Persons in Households	12,671	92.9
Householder	8,069	59.2
Spouse	1,757	12.9
Child	1,338	9.8
Own Child Under 18 Years	1,047	7.7
Other Relatives	254	1.9
Non Relatives	1,253	9.2
Non-rel Under 18	23	0.2
Non-rel Over 65	85	0.6

89   Appendix B - 2010 US Census Data   Straub Park - 1-mile radius

Subject	Number	Percent
Unmarried Partner	NA	
6. Households by Type		
Universe: Households		
Total Households	8,069	
Family Households (Families)	2,259	28.0
With Own Children Under 18 Years	642	8.0
Married Couple Family	1,757	21.8
With Own Children Under 18 Years	383	4.7
Female householder, No Husband Present	351	4.3
With Own Children Under 18 Years	195	2.4
Non Family Households	5,810	72.0
Unmarried Partner Households	NA	
Same-Sex Unmarried Partner HHs	NA	
Householder Living Alone	4,845	60.0
Householder 65 Years and Over	2,156	26.7
Households With Individuals Under 18 Years	688	8.5
7. Group Quarters		
Universe: Population Living in Group Quarters		
Population in Group Quarters	963	7.1
Institutionalized Population	75	0.6
Pop In Correctional Institutions	0	0.0
Pop in Nursing Homes	75	0.6
Pop in Other Institutions	0	0.0
NonInstitutionalized GQ Pop	888	6.5
College Dormitories (Includes college quarters off	331	2.4
Military Quarters	78	0.6
Other NonInstitutional GQ Pop	479	3.5
8. Housing Occupancy and Tenure		
Universe: Housing Units		
Total Housing Units	10,390	
Occupied Housing Units	8,069	77.7
Owner Occupied	2,928	36.3
Renter Occupied	5,141	63.7
Vacant Housing Units	2,321	22.3
Vacant for Rent	963	9.3
Vacant for Sale	271	2.6
Vacant for Seasonal,Recreation or Occasional Use	693	6.7
Homeowner Vacancy Rate	8.47	
Rental Vacancy Rate	15.78	

Subject	Number	Percent
Pop in Owner-occupied Units	5,490	40.3
Pop in Rented Units	7,181	52.7
Average Size of Owner-occupied Units	1.88	
Average Size of Renter-Occupied Units	1.40	

Note: *Varibles showing "NA" are not available at the blocks level. Specify tracts as the units to be aggregated to get values for these vars.*

Summary of true areas of circles vs. that of areas selected to estimate them

This report indicates how well we were able to approximate the circular area.

Radius	Estimated	True area	Ratio of estimate to true area
1	3.30	3.14	1.050

Auxiliary report: Counties contributing to circular areas, by concentric ring areas

Coordinates: 27.775458, -82.631460

Outer radius of ring (or circle)=1

County Cd	Total population
Pinellas FL	13,634
	13,634

See the CAPS index page for other versions of this program.

The **Missouri Census Data Center** is a Premier Local Partner of the U.S. Census Bureau and a sponsored program of the Missouri State Library.

Site published by the University of Missouri Office of Social and Economic Data Analysis. Please send comments/questions about this site to Glenn Rice (riceg@missouri.edu).

Circular Area Profiles

Missouri Census Data Center

Circular Area Profiles (CAPS) — 2010

Using data from Summary File 1, 2010 Census

Request details:

- Center point name:
- Latitude **27.767985**
- Longitude **-82.653286**
- Selected radii: **1**

[CSV file of aggregated data]

1-mile radius of specified point

Subject	Number	Percent
1. Total Population Trends, Etc.		
Universe: Total Population		
Total Population	13,586	
Total Population 2000	14,488	
Change in Population 2000-2010	-902	-6.2
Males	6,987	51.4
Females	6,599	48.6
Population Density	4287	
Land Area Sq. Miles	3	
2. Age		
Universe: Population		
Under 5 Years	854	6.3
Age 5 to 9 Years	651	4.8
10 to 14 Years	671	4.9
15 to 17 Years	467	3.4
18 to 19 Years	336	2.5
20 to 24 Years	947	7.0
25 to 34 Years	1,956	14.4
35 to 44 Years	1,953	14.4
45 to 54 Years	2,183	16.1
55 to 59 Years	912	6.7
Age 60 to 64 Years	734	5.4
65 to 74 Years	1,016	7.5

Subject	Number	Percent
75 to 84 Years	634	4.7
85 Years and Over	272	2.0
Median Age	39.0	
Age 0 to 17	2,643	19.5
18 to 24 Years	1,283	9.4
25 to 44 Years	3,909	28.8
45 to 64 Years	3,829	28.2
62 Years and Over	2,353	17.3
65 Years and Over	1,922	14.1
3. Race		
Universe: Population		
One Race	13,228	97.4
White	5,765	42.4
Black or African American	7,056	51.9
American Indian and Alaska Native	45	0.3
Asian	163	1.2
Native Hawaiian and Other Pacific Islander	1	0.0
Some Other Race	198	1.5
Multi Race - Persons reporting more than one race	358	2.6
4. Hispanic or Latino and Race		
Universe: Hispanic or Latino Population		
Hispanic or Latino (of any race)	747	5.5
Mexican	NA	
Puerto Rican	NA	
Cuban	NA	
Other Hispanic or Latino	NA	
Not Hispanic or Latino	12,839	94.5
White Alone Not Hispanic	5,374	39.6
5. Relationship of Persons in Households		
Universe: Persons in Households		
Total Persons in Households	12,313	90.6
Householder	6,173	45.4
Spouse	882	6.5
Child	2,947	21.7
Own Child Under 18 Years	1,984	14.6
Other Relatives	1,106	8.1
Non Relatives	1,205	8.9
Non-rel Under 18	62	0.5
Non-rel Over 65	47	0.3

Tropicana Field - 1-mile radius

Subject	Number	Percent
Unmarried Partner	NA	
6. Households by Type		
Universe: Households		
Total Households	6,173	
Family Households (Families)	2,379	38.5
With Own Children Under 18 Years	1,016	16.5
Married Couple Family	882	14.3
With Own Children Under 18 Years	254	4.1
Female householder, No Husband Present	1,217	19.7
With Own Children Under 18 Years	645	10.4
Non Family Households	3,794	61.5
Unmarried Partner Households	NA	
Same-Sex Unmarried Partner HHs	NA	
Householder Living Alone	3,118	50.5
Householder 65 Years and Over	1,519	24.6
Households With Individuals Under 18 Years	1,308	21.2
7. Group Quarters		
Universe: Population Living in Group Quarters		
Population in Group Quarters	1,273	9.4
Institutionalized Population	189	1.4
Pop In Correctional Institutions	32	0.2
Pop in Nursing Homes	157	1.2
Pop in Other Institutions	0	0.0
NonInstitutionalized GQ Pop	1,084	8.0
College Dormitories (Includes college quarters off	0	0.0
Military Quarters	0	0.0
Other NonInstitutional GQ Pop	1,084	8.0
8. Housing Occupancy and Tenure		
Universe: Housing Units		
Total Housing Units	8,277	
Occupied Housing Units	6,173	74.6
Owner Occupied	1,855	30.1
Renter Occupied	4,318	69.9
Vacant Housing Units	2,104	25.4
Vacant for Rent	847	10.2
Vacant for Sale	138	1.7
Vacant for Seasonal,Recreation or Occasional Use	53	0.6
Homeowner Vacancy Rate	6.92	
Rental Vacancy Rate	16.40	

Subject	Number	Percent
Pop in Owner-occupied Units	4,234	31.2
Pop in Rented Units	8,079	59.5
Average Size of Owner-occupied Units	2.28	
Average Size of Renter-Occupied Units	1.87	

Note: *Varibles showing "NA" are not available at the blocks level. Specify tracts as the units to be aggregated to get values for these vars.*

Summary of true areas of circles vs. that of areas selected to estimate them

This report indicates how well we were able to approximate the circular area.

Radius	Estimated	True area	Ratio of estimate to true area
1	3.19	3.14	1.014

Auxiliary report: Counties contributing to circular areas, by concentric ring areas

Coordinates: 27.767985, -82.653286

Outer radius of ring (or circle)=1

County Cd	Total population
Pinellas FL	13,586
	13,586

See the CAPS index page for other versions of this program.

Circular Area Profiles (CAPS) — ACS

Using data from 5-year period estimates, vintage 2016

Request details:

- Center point name:
- Latitude **27.775458**
- Longitude **-82.631460**
- Selected radii: **1**

1-mile radius of specified point

- **679** housing units were sampled (about 6.4%)
- **1,047** persons were sampled (about 7.6%)

Subject	Number	Percent
D1. AGE		
Universe:		
Total population	13,709	
Under 5 years	354	2.6
5 to 9 years	363	2.7
10 to 14 years	346	2.5
15 to 19 years	398	2.9
20 to 24 years	770	5.6
25 to 34 years	2,174	15.9
35 to 44 years	1,559	11.4
45 to 54 years	2,265	16.5
55 to 59 years	1,265	9.2
60 to 64 years	957	7.0
65 to 74 years	1,845	13.5
75 to 84 years	830	6.1
85 years and over	582	4.3
Median age in years	48.5	
5 years and over	N	97.4
15 years and over	12,645	92.2
Under 18 years of age	1,280	9.3
18 years and over	12,429	90.7

Subject	Number	Percent
21 years and over	12,040	87.8
25 years and over	11,476	83.7
62 years and over	3,782	27.6
65 years and over	3,257	23.8
D2. AGE AND SEX		
Universe:		
Total population	13,709	
Male	6,661	48.6
18 years old and over	N	92.4
65 years old and over	1,413	21.2
Female	7,048	51.4
18 years old and over	N	89.0
65 years old and over	1,845	26.2
D3. RACE		
Universe:		
Total population	13,709	
One race	13,420	97.9
White alone	12,011	87.6
Black or African American	1,119	8.2
American Indian and Alaska Native	25	0.2
Asian	172	1.2
Native Hawaiian and Other Pacific Islander	0	0.0
Some other race	93	0.7
Two or more races	289	2.1
White (alone or in combination)	12,273	89.5
Black (alone or in combination)	1,248	9.1
American Indian (alone or in combination)	84	0.6
Asian (alone or in combination)	261	1.9
Native Hawaiian (alone or in combination)	0	0.0
Some other race (alone or in combination)	134	1.0
D4. HISPANIC OR LATINO (ANY RACE)		
Universe:		
Total population	13,709	
Hispanic or Latino of any race	1,209	8.8
Not Hispanic or Latino	12,500	91.2
White alone	10,998	80.2
Black or African American alone	1,075	7.8
American Indian and Alaska Native alone	25	0.2
Asian alone	163	1.2

Subject	Number	Percent
Native Hawaiian and Other Pacific Islander alone	0	0.0
E1. HOUSEHOLD INCOME AND BENEFITS		
Universe:		
Total households	8,196	
Less than $10,000	1,016	12.4
$10,000 to $14,999	671	8.2
$15,000 to $24,999	1,129	13.8
$25,000 to $34,999	995	12.1
$35,000 to $49,999	874	10.7
$50,000 to $74,999	980	11.9
$75,000 to $99,999	555	6.8
$100,000 to $149,999	938	11.4
$150,000 to $199,999	506	6.2
$200,000 or more	533	6.5
With earnings	5,313	64.8
With social security	2,856	34.8
With retirement income	1,297	15.8
With supplemental security income	352	4.3
With cash public assistance income	197	2.4
With food stamp benefits in the past 12 months	N	N
Median household income	$48,491	
Mean household income	$76,281	
Mean household earnings	$84,800	
Mean household social security income	$17,868	
Mean household retirement income	$36,507	
Mean household supplemental security income	$7,739	
Mean household cash public assistance income	$1,008	
E2. FAMILY INCOME AND BENEFITS		
Universe: Total households		
Family households	2,348	28.7
Less than $10,000	84	3.6
$10,000 to $14,999	26	1.1
$15,000 to $24,999	68	2.9
$25,000 to $34,999	181	7.7
$35,000 to $49,999	157	6.7
$50,000 to $74,999	355	15.1
$75,000 to $99,999	201	8.6
$100,000 to $149,999	487	20.7
$150,000 to $199,999	361	15.4

Subject	Number	Percent
$200,000 or more	426	18.2
Median family income	N	
Mean family income	$152,841	
E3. OTHER INCOME MEASURES		
Universe:		
Per-capita income	$46,817	
Nonfamily households	5,848	71.3
Median nonfamily income	$30,977	
Mean nonfamily income	$45,371	
All full-time workers	N	
All male full-time workers	N	N
All female full-time workers	N	N
Median earnings for workers	N	
Median earnings for male full-time, year-round workers	N	
Median earnings for female full-time, year-round workers	N	
E4. POVERTY STATUS OVER THE LAST 12 MONTHS		
Universe:		
Persons for whom poverty status is determined	1,690	
Persons below poverty	2,356	17.7
Persons under 18 for whom poverty status is determined	N	
Persons under 18 in poverty	N	N
Persons aged 18 to 64 for whom poverty status is determined	N	
Persons aged 18 to 64 in poverty	N	N
Persons over 65 for whom poverty status is determined	N	
Persons over 65 in poverty	N	
Persons in families for whom poverty status is determined	6,231	N
Unrelated individuals for whom poverty status is determined	N	
Persons in families in poverty	584	9.4
Family households in poverty	166	7.1
Unrelated persons in poverty 15 years and over	N	N
Poverty ratio under 0.5	1,138	8.5
Poverty ratio in 0.5 to 0.99	1,219	9.1
Poverty ratio in 1 to 2	2,053	15.4
Poverty ratio in 2 and over	8,923	66.9
E5. EMPLOYMENT STATUS		
Universe:		
Population 16 years and over	12,614	
In labor force	7,501	725.6
Civilian labor force	7,421	718.3

Subject	Number	Percent
Employed civilians	6,952	1172
Unemployed civilians	469	68.0
In military	79	7.1
Not in labor force	5,114	514.7
Females 16 years and over	N	N
Females in labor force	N	N
Females in civilian labor force	N	N
Employed females	N	N
E6. CHILDREN WITH ALL PARENTS WORKING		
Universe:		
(Own) children under 6	418	
All parents working	246	58.9
(Own) children aged 6 to 17	784	
All parents working	457	58.3
E7. COMMUTING TO WORK		
Universe:		
Workers 16 years and over	6,907	
Workers 16+ who commute to work	6,182	89.5
Car, truck, or van; drove alone	4,819	69.8
Car, truck, or van; carpooled	374	5.4
Public transportation (excluding taxicab)	176	2.6
Walked to work	361	5.2
Other means of commuting	452	6.5
Worked at home	725	10.5
Mean travel time to work in minutes	N	

Data used in this report is from the American Community Survey 5-year period estimates data for 2012-2016 . This metadata report provides some background information on the data items appearing in the report. Block Group-level data were used with the BBIA algorithm for apportioning data to the circular areas.

See the CAPS index page for other versions of this program.

The **Missouri Census Data Center** is a Premier Local Partner of the U.S. Census Bureau and a sponsored program of the Missouri State Library.

Site published by the University of Missouri Office of Social and Economic Data Analysis.

Please send comments/questions about this site to Glenn Rice (riceg@missouri.edu).

Circular Area Profiles (CAPS) — ACS

Using data from 5-year period estimates, vintage 2016

Request details:

- Center point name:
- Latitude **27.767985**
- Longitude **-82.653286**
- Selected radii: **1**

1-mile radius of specified point

- **657** housing units were sampled (about 8.0%)
- **1,064** persons were sampled (about 7.8%)

Subject	Number	Percent
D1. AGE		
Universe:		
Total population	13,719	
Under 5 years	594	4.3
5 to 9 years	569	4.2
10 to 14 years	728	5.3
15 to 19 years	733	5.3
20 to 24 years	1,342	9.8
25 to 34 years	1,988	14.5
35 to 44 years	1,963	14.3
45 to 54 years	1,806	13.2
55 to 59 years	1,113	8.1
60 to 64 years	911	6.6
65 to 74 years	1,231	9.0
75 to 84 years	547	4.0
85 years and over	194	1.4
Median age in years	40.3	
5 years and over	N	95.7
15 years and over	11,829	86.2
Under 18 years of age	2,252	16.4
18 years and over	11,467	83.6

	Number	Percent
21 years and over	10,789	78.7
25 years and over	9,754	71.1
62 years and over	2,510	18.3
65 years and over	1,972	14.4
D2. AGE AND SEX		
Universe:		
Total population	13,719	
Male	6,918	50.4
18 years old and over	N	82.9
65 years old and over	879	12.7
Female	6,801	49.6
18 years old and over	N	84.2
65 years old and over	1,093	16.1
D3. RACE		
Universe:		
Total population	13,719	
One race	13,338	97.2
White alone	6,736	49.1
Black or African American	6,213	45.3
American Indian and Alaska Native	14	0.1
Asian	264	1.9
Native Hawaiian and Other Pacific Islander	4	0.0
Some other race	108	0.8
Two or more races	380	2.8
White (alone or in combination)	7,062	51.5
Black (alone or in combination)	6,513	47.5
American Indian (alone or in combination)	109	0.8
Asian (alone or in combination)	318	2.3
Native Hawaiian (alone or in combination)	6	0.0
Some other race (alone or in combination)	130	1.0
D4. HISPANIC OR LATINO (ANY RACE)		
Universe:		
Total population	13,719	
Hispanic or Latino of any race	1,319	9.6
Not Hispanic or Latino	12,400	90.4
White alone	5,580	40.7
Black or African American alone	6,204	45.2
American Indian and Alaska Native alone	14	0.1
Asian alone	262	1.9

	Number	Percent
Native Hawaiian and Other Pacific Islander alone	4	0.0
E1. HOUSEHOLD INCOME AND BENEFITS		
Universe:		
Total households	6,329	
Less than $10,000	1,234	19.5
$10,000 to $14,999	648	10.2
$15,000 to $24,999	1,018	16.1
$25,000 to $34,999	835	13.2
$35,000 to $49,999	842	13.3
$50,000 to $74,999	799	12.6
$75,000 to $99,999	354	5.6
$100,000 to $149,999	398	6.3
$150,000 to $199,999	97	1.5
$200,000 or more	104	1.6
With earnings	3,988	63.0
With social security	2,031	32.1
With retirement income	720	11.4
With supplemental security income	706	11.2
With cash public assistance income	331	5.2
With food stamp benefits in the past 12 months	N	N
Median household income	$30,678	
Mean household income	$43,455	
Mean household earnings	$52,292	
Mean household social security income	$13,291	
Mean household retirement income	$18,104	
Mean household supplemental security income	$7,994	
Mean household cash public assistance income	$2,665	
E2. FAMILY INCOME AND BENEFITS		
Universe: Total households		
Family households	2,170	34.3
Less than $10,000	355	16.4
$10,000 to $14,999	119	5.5
$15,000 to $24,999	225	10.4
$25,000 to $34,999	291	13.4
$35,000 to $49,999	287	13.2
$50,000 to $74,999	422	19.4
$75,000 to $99,999	147	6.8
$100,000 to $149,999	198	9.1
$150,000 to $199,999	52	2.4

Tropicana Field – 1-mile radius

	Number	Percent
$200,000 or more	74	3.4
Median family income	N	
Mean family income	$58,401	
E3. OTHER INCOME MEASURES		
Universe:		
Per-capita income	$21,726	
Nonfamily households	4,160	65.7
Median nonfamily income	$25,706	
Mean nonfamily income	$35,322	
All full-time workers	N	
All male full-time workers	N	N
All female full-time workers	N	N
Median earnings for workers	N	
Median earnings for male full-time, year-round workers	N	
Median earnings for female full-time, year-round workers	N	
E4. POVERTY STATUS OVER THE LAST 12 MONTHS		
Universe:		
Persons for whom poverty status is determined	959	
Persons below poverty	4,408	33.2
Persons under 18 for whom poverty status is determined	N	
Persons under 18 in poverty	N	N
Persons aged 18 to 64 for whom poverty status is determined	N	
Persons aged 18 to 64 in poverty	N	N
Persons over 65 for whom poverty status is determined	N	
Persons over 65 in poverty	N	N
Persons in families for whom poverty status is determined	7,416	N
Unrelated individuals for whom poverty status is determined	N	
Persons in families in poverty	2,219	29.9
Family households in poverty	603	27.8
Unrelated persons in poverty 15 years and over	N	N
Poverty ratio under 0.5	2,315	17.4
Poverty ratio in 0.5 to 0.99	2,092	15.8
Poverty ratio in 1 to 2	3,253	24.5
Poverty ratio in 2 and over	5,616	42.3
E5. EMPLOYMENT STATUS		
Universe:		
Population 16 years and over	11,731	
In labor force	6,568	890.1
Civilian labor force	6,533	886.3

	Number	Percent
Employed civilians	5,811	1420
Unemployed civilians	722	167.0
In military	35	3.8
Not in labor force	5,163	696.9
Females 16 years and over	N	N
Females in labor force	N	N
Females in civilian labor force	N	N
Employed females	N	N
E6. CHILDREN WITH ALL PARENTS WORKING		
Universe:		
(Own) children under 6	699	
All parents working	484	69.2
(Own) children aged 6 to 17	1,342	
All parents working	1,093	81.5
E7. COMMUTING TO WORK		
Universe:		
Workers 16 years and over	5,726	
Workers 16+ who commute to work	5,544	96.8
Car, truck, or van; drove alone	4,184	73.1
Car, truck, or van; carpooled	315	5.5
Public transportation (excluding taxicab)	454	7.9
Walked to work	301	5.2
Other means of commuting	290	5.1
Worked at home	182	3.2
Mean travel time to work in minutes	N	

Data used in this report is from the American Community Survey 5-year period estimates data for 2012-2016 . This metadata report provides some background information on the data items appearing in the report. Block Group-level data were used with the BBIA algorithm for apportioning data to the circular areas.

See the CAPS index page for other versions of this program.

The **Missouri Census Data Center** is a Premier Local Partner of the U.S. Census Bureau and a sponsored program of the Missouri State Library.

Site published by the University of Missouri Office of Social and Economic Data Analysis.
Please send comments/questions about this site to Glenn Rice (riceg@missouri.edu).

93   Bibliography

Bachelard, G., & Bachelard, S. (1990). Fragments of a Poetics of Fire. Dallas, TX: Dallas Institute Publications

Badger E., (July 16th, 2015)), How railroads, highways, and other man-made lines racially divide America's cities, The Washington Post

Benfield K., July 12th, 2012, The Park at the Forefront of Cincinnati's Revitalization, Citylab,
https://www.citylab.com/design/2012/07/park-forefront-cincinnatis-revitalization/2557/

Brown M. (Aug 8th, 2016), The secrets to landing a MLB Expansion Team, Forbes Magazine.

Cheonggye Freeway, Congress for the New Urbanism, https://www.cnu.org/what-we-do/build-great-places/cheonggye-freeway

D'Alessio E., (February 18th, 2016), Piazza del Campo, Project for Public Spaces, https://www.pps.org/places/piazza-del-campo

Glasser E., (February 9th, 2018), People Forced Out When Trop Was Built Still Resentful, WTSP,
https://www.wtsp.com/article/sports/mlb/rays/people-forced-out-when-trop-was-built-still-resentful/67-516868751

Gregor A., (April 8th, 2015) Sugar Hill: Rich in Culture and Affordable, New York Times.

Harper J., (29 March 1998), Around the Dome, Echoes of the Past. St. Petersburg Times.

Harvey D., (2003) The right to the city. International Journal of Urban and Regional Research, 27: 939-941

Hensley D. (April 2011), History of the Orange Line, Trains Magazine.

"I-275 south feeder is open downtown.", (July 24, 1980), St. Petersburg Times.

Jacobs J., (2004), Dark Age Ahead, New York, Vintage Books.

Jacobs J., (1961), The Death and Life of Great American Cities, New York, Random House.

Leinberger C. & Loh T., (May 2018) Catalytic development: (Re)creating Walkable Urban Places, Brookings Institution.
https://www.brookings.edu/wp-content/uploads/2018/05/brookings-180420-catalytic-development-paper_may-2018-final.pdf

Levy B. (2012) Urban Square as the Place of History, Memory, Identity,
n: Dusica Drazic, Slavica Radisic, Marijana Simu (eds), Memory of the City, Kulturklammer, Belgrade, 156-173

Mapping Inequality - Redlining in New Deal America, University of Richmond, VA
https://dsl.richmond.edu/panorama/redlining/#loc=11/27.7760/-82.6765&opacity=0.8&city=st.petersburg-fl

Marcus, C. C., & Francis, C. (1997). People places: Design guidelines for Urban Open Space. New York: John Wiley & Sons.

Memluk M., (July 1st, 2013), Designing Urban Squares, Advances in Landscape Architecture.

Moore W.A, (April 19th, 2019), St. Petersburg approves plan to preserve small storefronts, Tampa Bay Times.

Moskowitz P. E., (2017) How to Kill a City, Gentrification, Inequality, and the Fight for the Neighborhood, New York, Nation Books.

Nickens T., (July 15th, 2016), Nickens: How two bets on the future define a city, Tampa Bay Times,
https://www.tampabay.com/opinion/columns/nickens-rays-vote-preserves-st-petersburg-legacy/2261514

Peck R, Wilson J. (2006) St. Petersburg's Historic 22nd Street South. Charleston, SC: History Press.

Peck R, Wilson J. (2008) St. Petersburg's historic African American neighborhoods. Charleston, SC: History Press; 2008.

Phelps T., (May 20, 1975), The James of Jamestown Faces Loss of Home There, St Petersburg Times

Project for Public Spaces, (November 30th, 2005), 10 Principles for Successful Squares,
https://www.pps.org/article/squaresprinciples

Project for Public Spaces, Campus Martius, https://www.pps.org/projects/campusmartius

Project for Public Spaces, Discovery Green: Houston's Backyard, https://www.pps.org/projects/houstonpark

Project for Public Spaces, Pittsburgh Market Square, https://www.pps.org/projects/pittsburgh-market-square

Project for Public Spaces, (July 22nd, 2015), Portsmouth Square, https://www.pps.org/places/portsmouth-square

Schilder F. and Scherpenisse R., (2018), Policy and Practice — Affordable Housing in the Netherlands,
https://www.pbl.nl/sites/default/files/cms/publicaties/PBL2018_Policy-and-practice-affordable-housing-in-the-Netherlands_3336.pdf

Schindler S., (April 2015) Architectural Exclusion: Discrimination and Segregation Through Physical Design of the Built Environment
Yale Law Journal, Vol 124 No. 6

Van Boom M., (July 9th, 2018), How the Dutch do Affordable Housing, Interfaith housing initiative

Walker M. (November 24, 1986), "Stadium Ground Broken". Boca Raton News, Pp 6C.

Wilson J., (April 17th, 2014), Jordan Park over the years, The Weekly Challenger.

Wright C., (April 14th, 2014), Historic Roser Park celebrates 100 years, Tampa Bay Times.